TIME *for* LIVING

TIME

for LIVING

BY GEORGE SOULE

THE VIKING PRESS

NEW YORK · 1955

COPYRIGHT © 1955 BY GEORGE SOULE

FIRST PUBLISHED BY THE VIKING PRESS IN SEPTEMBER 1955

PUBLISHED ON THE SAME DAY IN THE DOMINION OF CANADA

BY THE MACMILLAN COMPANY OF CANADA LIMITED

Dec. 27. 1955
089

$3.00

Library of Congress catalog card: 55-9785

PRINTED IN U.S.A. BY VAIL-BALLOU PRESS, INC.

FOR MY FRIENDS

OF BENNINGTON COLLEGE

CONTENTS

vii

TIME *for* LIVING

1

A TECHNOLOGICAL
CIVILIZATION

Biologists have a word for an insect in any one of the forms which it assumes between successive molts—*instar*. An egg is an instar, a larva or pupa of the same individual is an instar, the full-fledged butterfly, fly, or beetle is an instar. To apply a beautiful and precise term like this where it does not belong is not fitting, but the temptation to steal it for describing human change is irresistible. A single person is successively fetus, infant, adolescent, adult. To be sure, the change from one of these stages to the next does not mark such marvelous differences as in the insect, nor is it so dramatically visible. Yet to call each stage by analogy an instar sharpens the observation that the person does indeed successively and periodically assume different embodiments and ways of living.

Something similar may be discerned in the changes which occur in Western civilization. These stages, though less easily identifiable than in the individual person, are clear enough in the large so that historians have given names to them and have attempted to describe their special characteristics. Medieval Europe after centuries of slow change gave way to the civilization now regarded as modern. The beginning of this transformation is often called "renaissance"—rebirth; at least it appears sudden and dramatic enough in retrospect so that it is seen as something more than mere gradual development.

The question which is briefly examined in this book is whether another rebirth into another instar may be in prospect. Sources of such a change may already be found, if one looks at familiar facts to see whether they fit the pattern of transformation from one instar in the social organization of mankind to another.

Those sources are in large part related to the process now a commonplace to most Americans—the advance of technology, by virtue of which this nation has achieved pre-eminence in material welfare. This gain is celebrated in every economic report, every homily on the virtues of free private enterprise. It is, we are told, the chief reason why the United States has become the richest and most powerful nation in the world. Other regions, "underdeveloped" or less well developed than ours, are urged to learn how it is done and follow the American example.

How could so humdrum an affair possibly have such momentous consequences as a transition to a different stage of civilization? To most of us technological advance seems to mean little more than new television sets, sleeker and faster cars, better washing machines, resplendent supermarkets, and a host of intriguing gadgets. But let us take a longer and deeper look at technology and its implications.

A revolution in technology was the core of the process which transformed the middle ages into the modern world. That whole process, to be sure, included other indispensable elements, such as new ideas, social mores, economic and political institutions. But how could the ideas have been broadcast so rapidly without the invention of printing and movable type? How could community life and government have changed as they did without trade and communication among provinces, nations, and continents? And how could trade have expanded without the improvement of roads, the construction of canals and railways, the invention of the mariner's compass? How could large urban populations, the base of modern civilization, have been fed without the birth of scientific agriculture, and how, without the surplus farm population—a surplus to which a renovated agriculture gave rise—could mills and factories have recruited their workers? And how could factory chimneys have cast their long shadows over civilization without the successive advances in the use of energy-transforming engines or the machinery which only great sources of mechanical power could activate?

To say all this is not to say that technological improvement is a fitting goal for the activities of man, or that it is even a goal at all. Rather it is a possible means to other ends. Nor is it to say that such values as liberty, the dignity of the individual, the democratization of government, the scientific method, and all the rest which flowered in the great transition are of no more worth than for filling bellies, protecting against cold and disease, or amusement of idle hours. Indeed, technological civilization has brought in its train much that is evil, such as that horrible invention of modern man, mechanized, atomic, and biological warfare, or that scarcely less corrupting force, mass communication, when it is dedicated to untruths or trivialities.

The transformation to modernism at its most rapid stage, in the late 1700s and early 1800s, has been christened the "industrial revolution." Factories substituting the power of falling water or steam for human muscle, and replacing skilled handicraftsmen with machines, did in sober truth turn methods of production upside down. In doing so they profoundly affected

all the rest of man's life wherever they prevailed. So familiar
is this theme that it is customary to regard the industrial
revolution as something that arrived, did its job, and then
settled down to a jog-trot far from revolutionary—at least in
the Western world.

But scientific discovery continued and technology did not
stop. The first coming of railroads and the factory system is
merely part of a broader and longer stream of technological
development which has embraced agriculture, mining, forestry, communication, trade, and other services. The changes
which it has made in civilization have broadened, deepened,
and have not yet reached their climax. Before we finish with
the industrial revolution, or, more properly, the technological
revolution, there may be required another revaluation in
thinking and customs similar to that which accompanied its
birth pangs.

There may arrive a maturity of modern civilization to succeed its infancy and adolescence. Or there may not. Yet surely
momentous change of some kind is occurring; a society har-
boring so restless and dynamic an impulse as the limitless
search of science and its infinite utilitarian applications can
scarcely settle down to a social order dreaming away the centuries in stagnation.

If one is to examine the technological spur to change in its
purest and most significant condition, one must look at it in the
United States. To be sure, it was in Western Europe that the
shift to modern methods and ways of thinking began, and the
industrial revolution itself became supreme in Britain before
America adopted it. Scientific discoveries and inventions have
occurred wherever men have learned to think in the modern
way; many of the "improvements" utilized west of the Atlantic
have been borrowed from east of it, though often applied in
the United States with somewhat greater verve and intensity.
Yet nowhere else could one find a so nearly wholehearted and
universal acceptance of the essence of the process; indeed,

belief in it may almost be said by now to have become a leading American myth. In no other culture, even in no other Western culture than that of the United States, is there so deep-seated a commitment to technical progress as a national virtue and as the salvation of mankind. Elsewhere, the myths which give meaning and coherence to life are likely to be of a different order.

It was not always so in what is now the United States. The early settlers, insofar as they came voluntarily and for material reasons, came in search of land and the sustenance that could be won from it, not of engines and machines. These things of course were not then common in the Europe which they left. Four-fifths of the American people were farmers or at least lived in rural regions long after mill towns began to smudge the English and Scottish countryside.

More than the peoples of older regions, Americans seemed, on the surface at least, to exercise deliberate choices as to how they would make their living and how they would live together. Adoption of the industrial revolution is no exception to this apparently rational approach. When Alexander Hamilton, as the first Secretary of the Treasury, issued his famous "Report on the Subject of Manufactures," he was not defending the interest of an existing and powerful manufacturing class, since there was none. He was concerned rather with convincing the nation that it was desirable to create a factory industry and with solving the difficult problem of doing so. His adversary in the great debate, Thomas Jefferson, opposed the adoption of factories and all that went with them, tacitly assuming that Americans could, if they liked, remain a rural, argricultural, and decentralized people. Neither supposed that what is now variously referred to as the industrial revolution or free private enterprise in business was an ineluctable and impersonal force, bound to prevail by its own dynamism if only governments would stand out of its way.

Hamilton in effect won the argument; government did give

positive encouragement to transportation and the factory system, and supported them by delegation of powers, by subsidies, and by tariffs. Individual Americans, as inhabitants of an "underdeveloped" country, chose to develop them and did develop them, through the application of intensive thinking, immense effort, and the sacrifices inevitably involved in taking risks and making mistakes.

Not for a hundred years or more did acceptance of the new industrial mode become widespread and ungrudging. Important parts of the community opposed or stood aside. Southern planters, after an unsuccessful attempt to make a go of cotton mills, pushed the protective tariff down and kept it low until after their defeat in the Civil War. Democrats of the agricultural frontier joined the forces that opposed federal planning and construction of canals and roads; they fought in the name of democracy against the early attempts at concentration of money power essential for investment in large enterprises and required for central banking. Agriculture was at odds with industry and finance on monetary policy, land policy, and regulation all through the latter part of the nineteenth century. Wage-workers, though only spasmodically organized, struggled against employers on dozens of issues. Though in the long run labor accepted the technological revolution in a broad sense, organizations of workers often tried to protect the skilled handicraftsman against degradation into a mere servant of the machine.

America was not immune to the conflicts which brought civil shocks to every community touched by the industrial revolution. Why, then, did technological industry not only flourish in the United States, but become accepted and glorified, instead of being merely tolerated, among other innovations, as in the regions of its birth? How great is the present difference among cultures in this respect few Americans appreciate, unless they have had occasion to explore the at-

titude of Europeans on the subject, not to speak of Latin
Americans and Asians.

No people is averse to having enough to eat and wear, none
is without groups desiring to accumulate riches, if that seems
possible. Aristocratic traditions, however, based in the first
instance on the outlook of landed proprietors, fighting men,
and priests, have always placed in the lower ranks both business pursued for gain and manual labor. Plato and Aristotle
expressed this view in ancient Greece. As much production as
was necessary for use could be justified, they held, and to trade
one useful article for another was legitimate. But money itself
was "sterile" except as a medium of exchange; to seek or to
hoard such unproductive wealth or to charge usury (interest)
for lending it was evil. Manual labor, though necessary, was a
brutalizing occupation unfit for citizens, who must be free to
devote their minds to public affairs. This tradition, in various
guises, survived in feudal Europe; it was not eliminated when
modern business and production eventually shoved aside the
feudal order.

In Britain aristocratic views were perpetuated by a partly
hereditary, partly professionalized governing class. Wave after
wave of democratization swept over the "nation of shopkeepers" without much tarnishing the ancient values. Successful manufacturers might be made peers of the realm, but it
was the realm, not success in manufacturing, that bestowed
on them their robes of distinction. The sons of businessmen,
after attending Oxford and Cambridge, might rise in politics,
diplomacy, professions, or the civil service, but as they rose
they cast business off and assumed something of the attitude
of *noblesse oblige*. Labor itself won governmental power, but
bowed to ancient decencies as its program was delivered as a
speech from the throne. The nation is full of great factories
and banks, just as a house may have its kitchen and its laundry,
but they are accepted as a matter of course rather than

glorified as the justification of national existence. Wealth exists
for use or for power. The process of making it is still felt by
many to be a bit untidy, to be kept out of sight when guests are
in the house, certainly not to be displayed and boasted of.

In France the aristocracy was subdued not by erosion as in
England, but by volcanic eruption. The bourgeoisie, the historians tell us, won the French Revolution, and they have remained on top ever since. The aristocratic tradition nevertheless got its revenge by making *bourgeois* almost a term of
ridicule, especially among the intellectuals and other free
spirits who flourish in France, and provide much of what both
Frenchmen and foreigners regard as the peculiar distinction
of the nation. Your typical Frenchman, if one may be allowed
to cite so mythological a being, bows to no authority; he is
not even comfortable in the discipline of political democracy,
with its need for majorities. What happened was not so much
that aristocracy was conquered by democrats as that democrats succeeded to aristocracy; everybody regards himself as
an aristocrat in his own right.

Nowhere has it been more difficult than in France for
American businessmen, with their missionary zeal in the European Cooperation Administration, to introduce more productive methods or to induce the acceptance of competition.
Many businesses are controlled by families who, living fairly
well on their existing profits, see no reason to spend large
amounts on new equipment when the old will do, or to produce more when additional production might break markets
and lower established prices. France often seems to have
settled down to enjoy the modest benefits of the early industrial revolution—or to quarrel over their division—without
putting her heart into an enterprising effort to push that
revolution to its limits.

Different assessments would be necessary for Germany,
Sweden, or Switzerland as shrewd adapters or innovators of
technology, or for Italy, a nation poor in resources though rich

in skills. Nowhere else in the Western world, however, could one find quite the single-minded dedication to more production with less labor that prevails in the United States. Nowhere else could one sense among nearly all classes and groups the positive enthusiasm for technological improvement almost as a thing to be desired in itself, aside from its utility for other purposes.

It may be idle to speculate on the reason for this difference in outlook. Perhaps it is the fact that America, its vast expanses of land calling for workers, could not for long provide a favorable setting for a landed aristocracy and its values. Perhaps the difference owes something to the fluid admixture of peoples from many nations and cultures, in which old-world values tended to be reduced to a common denominator —the right of every man to strive for the best the nation could afford, and an unusual opportunity for him to achieve it.

My suspicion, however, is that the reason runs somewhat deeper than this. The nation was dedicated to a new civilization unhampered by European inhibitions. What could be fresher than the discoveries of science and their application in technology—a continuous stream of newness in tangible and immediate form? Every new gadget is a symbol, however unworthy, of the original dedication. It is more than something curious or useful; it is a visible sign of the faith that is believed to work miracles.

Even Jefferson, who opposed the industrial revolution largely on the aristocratic ground that illiterate, propertyless, and exploited factory workers in ugly cities would be unfit citizens of a democracy, was himself a distinguished devotee of science and an inventor of no mean skill. He designed the modern iron plow. It was President Jefferson and members of his Cabinet who sanctioned use of mass production—perhaps the first use in the world—when they permitted Eli Whitney to fulfill his government contract for muskets by the fabrication and assembly of interchangeable parts. Americans felt the fascination of ingenuity and the desirability of economizing time and labor even in the early 1800s, and have continued to feel them ever since. Whatever fears Jefferson and later citizens have entertained concerning the social outcome of new methods of production, they have never failed to embrace the technological changes which make these methods possible.

The ordinary American assumes, not that each new invention is guilty until proved innocent, but that it is good in itself. If evil results follow, they are thought incidental, and possible to banish without hampering the source of change. Businessmen may make careful calculation of cost savings when they install new equipment, but underlying such thrifty planning is the deep conviction that the main current of technological civilization enforces continual change and that anyone who does not advance with it will perish. An examination of the present process of change which depends on technology may therefore with benefit be centered on the United States as the most eminent example.

If searching questions were directed to Americans concerning the worth of this process of change, they might find difficulty in giving an ultimately satisfactory reply. Does man's nature demand change more than security or serenity? Is it safe to assume that any change is for the better? Change in itself may occasionally be stimulating, but it is as frequently uncomfortable or even destructive. Is it a law of nature that man's ingenuity can lead only to improvement of his condition? The common justification of high and increasing productivity is that it is capable of providing more necessary or more desirable things and services for more people. But did men and women of former centuries who had fewer things and services necessarily have less happy or less fruitful lives? And what is the merit of sustaining more people and helping them to live longer unless those who are added to the population lead a more fully human life? Employment is surely preferable to unemployment, but what is the ultimate worth of the products which the fully employed fabricate? Questions like these lurk in the minds, even if not in the words, of people in the rest of the world who are urged to serve themselves by following the American example. A belief that contemporary Americans have not answered such questions contributes to the distrust or dislike with which many citizens of other nations regard the contemporary spirit of the United States.

Nobody questions that the power of the United States is very great. Its military prowess has been proved in recent wars; the economic bulk which forms the essential basis of that prowess is equally impressive in time of peace for its capacity to do good or evil. Let the United States prosper, and other nations can more easily solve their difficulties; let the United States suffer even a minor depression, and their economic structures tremble. The powerful cannot expect to be too much liked, however much they must perforce be respected.

Americans are acknowledged to be generous—with their tangible wealth and often with their time and effort. But appreciation for American material generosity is often combined with fear that the distantly related but quite different quality, magnanimity, is too little in evidence. To be generous in the realm of the mind and to be humble in spirit is a rare virtue anywhere, but those with great power can do with more of it than those whom there is no reason to fear.

No nation can with dignity govern its action by the opinion of others. But any nation, like any person, may benefit by seeing itself occasionally through others' eyes. Do Americans themselves know in what direction they are going? Do they understand what it is they are striving to protect from internal and external danger? Answers to such questions, to be sure, are intangible and difficult to put into words. Sometimes, however, it appears that the most valiant warriors for "Americanism" are, unlike great Americans at previous times of crisis, more concerned to cherish the past than to work out a vision of the future. There could be no greater betrayal of the national tradition than this.

If this nation is now distinguished from others by its successful dedication to technological advance more than by anything else, it would be well to question where that dedication is leading, not just tomorrow or next year, but in the more distant future. Are there now, or will there be, new occasions for rational choices of grand policy such as were recognized and debated by Americans of former centuries? Are the great controversies that accompanied the beginning and the middle course of the industrial revolution forever stilled? Perhaps it would be well to shut off the television set, leave the car in the garage, and silence the telephone long enough to engage in a little speculative reflection about the future of the civilization of which technological advance has turned out to be at once the motive power and the visible symbol.

2

THE EXPLODING CURVE

The technological revolution has given man in the middle years of the twentieth century many things of which his great-grandfathers and great-grandmothers never dreamed. At this stage of the inquiry it would be pointless to elaborate a matter of such common knowledge. For the present let us examine briefly another aspect of the process that is more intimately characteristic of advancing technology—the continual gain in ability to produce more in a given time. Or, to state the same observation in another way, to produce the same amount in less time.

This gain began with the industrial revolution itself. When the early textile mills put men and women to work at spinning jennies and, later, at power looms, they were able to produce so much more yarn and cloth with a given expenditure of labor hours that they quickly put most of the hand spinners and weavers out of business. This procedure has spread from

industry to industry and from operation to operation. It was
not possible to measure the national productive gain until recently; indeed, the figures on the basis of which a respectable
estimate could be made did not begin to be gathered until
the late nineteenth century. Nevertheless it certainly occurred.

Recent Productive Gains

A skillful statistician of the National Bureau of Economic
Research, Frederick C. Mills, recently put some of these
figures together. The following summary is based upon his
calculations. Other estimators have found much the same
result.

Everything produced and sold in the United States, including both goods and services, can be lumped together by stating
it in terms of its dollar value. That sum is called Gross National
Product. In order to find how the Gross National Product has
increased, it is desirable to modify the money total for changes
in the purchasing power of the dollar. When that has been
done, the sum is called *Real* Gross National Product. Mr.
Mills found that the Real Gross National Product had become
a little more than five times as great in the decade 1941–1950
as in the decade 1891–1900.

This gain includes everything bought or sold—not merely
the output of factories but the production of the machinery
they use, the construction of the factories themselves and of all
other buildings and houses, the railroads and their services, the
roads, ships, and airlines, the services of wholesalers and re-
tailers, the contributions of the lumbermen, fishermen, and
farmers, the output of mines, the work of teachers, postmen,
and all other government employees, the services of doctors,
lawyers, and so on.

While the total product was growing fivefold, the population merely doubled. That means, roughly, that the intake of

the population could have been two and one-half times larger *per person* in the middle of the twentieth century than in the last decade of the nineteenth. Still more striking is a fact with which at this point we are specially concerned—that while the gross output quintupled, the total labor hours required to produce it increased only about 80 per cent. In consequence, the *output per man-hour* was 181 per cent greater in 1941–1950 than in 1891–1900. That is, the average worker, in one hour's work, was able to produce between two and three times as much at the end of the half-century as he had at the beginning—and more nearly thrice than twice as much.

Mr. Mills made a rough but interesting calculation to see what happened to the gains in production. (His figures are all stated in dollars that could buy the same amount as in 1929.) In the decade 1941–1950, for example, $803 billion was needed to support the population at the level to which it was accustomed. To maintain the capital of the country by replacing worn-out buildings and machinery required another $132 billion. That left $558 billion extra—a "margin above maintenance" that could be used for other purposes. How was it used, as a matter of fact?

$285 billion was used to increase what individuals consumed.

$228 billion was used for war and defense.

$45 billion was used to increase the capital, in other words, the productive equipment, of the nation.

The margin above maintenance varied widely from one decade to another, and its uses varied even more widely. In the depression years 1931–1940 there occurred an actual decrease in consumption amounting to $9 billion; and a net capital increase of only $12 billion, while $11 billion went to augment war and defense. In 1921–1930, for the most part prosperous years, consumers gained $140 billion, capital grew $75 billion, and war received only $8 billion of the surplus. In

1911–1920, the time of World War I, net capital increase topped both the amounts spent for war and the additions to consumption.

An obvious conclusion drawn from facts such as these is that because of increase in output per man-hour the consumers of the United States—and everybody is a consumer—could improve their living levels more rapidly if it were not for depressions and wars. Nevertheless, even with depressions and wars, the improvement has been spectacular.

Projecting the Trend

Summarizing more extensive studies, Solomon Fabricant, Director of Research of the National Bureau of Economic Research, wrote in his annual report for 1954 that there had been an average annual increase of 1.9 per cent for the eighty years before 1950 in what is called the per capita real income of the people of the United States. Per capita income is an inelegant term for the result obtained when the total national money income is divided by the number of people in the population. Real income means merely that the effect of price changes is eliminated, so that shifting values of the dollar do not show up in the figures.

This average 1.9 per cent annual gain does not actually apply to every year or to every individual. In some years the gain is more, in some less; and not everyone invariably gets his share of the advance. In any one year even the average gain may seem slight. Which of us would much notice an increase of 1.9 per cent in his income? Yet the regular recurrence of this gain piles up. It is what brought the average income per family in the United States to a little more than $5000 in 1953. What is more striking, this annual gain will, if it continues, bring the average income per family to $25,000 (in 1953 dollars) during the next eighty years—in time for our grandchildren or great-grandchildren to enjoy that luxury. Families with incomes of $25,000 or more now make up only the top 1 per cent of the population.

A generation or two is not a long time in the life of the nation; let us look farther ahead and suppose that the growth observed over the past eighty years continues indefinitely. When even so small an amount as $2 is added year after year to every $100, what happens is familiar to all who know about compound interest. The longer interest is regularly added to a given amount of savings in the bank, the faster those savings grow, even if the depositor never saves any more. Leave the money alone long enough and it will become fantastically large. If we should chart a gain of this kind—and the increase in per capita national income is a gain of this kind—the graph would look something like this:

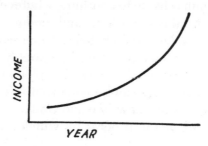

This kind of curve shows an accelerating growth. It is sometimes called an "exploding" curve, because it goes off into vertical space without ever turning back. If used to picture economic production, the curve signifies that though income per person grows moderately at the beginning of the process, it approaches more and more rapidly (though it will never quite attain) the point where it would be possible for every individual in the nation *to have so much that it would be immeasurable—that is, an infinite amount of goods and services.*

Such a progression could not continue for very long without being accompanied by remarkable changes in the way men

live. If, as almost everyone now believes, there is to be no
halt in the headlong pace of accelerating technology, and if it
may be expected to continue indefinitely, the explosion of the
technological curve is likely to necessitate stupendous revalua-
tions in present hopes, fears, goals, and measures of worth.

Will the Gain in Income Continue?

Predictions based on projection of statistical curves into
the future are notoriously unreliable. The future is almost
always surprising, and it often surprises those who have carefully calculated what will happen as much as it does those who
heedlessly suppose that the next year, or the next decade, will
be just like the last one. Yet it is important to guess whether
technological gain is likely to continue, whatever the outcome
may be. For if it did not continue, and income should remain
stable or even diminish, the changes which would be neces-
sitated in American society would be scarcely less imposing
than if the technological curve should explode into incredible
plenty. Either way, there can be no perpetuation of the manner in which Americans now live and think. Let us therefore
have a closer look at the process by which gains in income
are produced.

The growth in income for a population of any given size
depends upon a number of factors, some tangible, some intangible. All of them can be reduced, for purposes of measurement, to two—the number of labor and capital units devoted
to production, and the output per unit.

The amount of labor available depends in part on the proportion of the population willing and able to work. A nation
which is so subject to disease or malnutrition that a large number die at an early age has proportionally fewer who can do
work than one in which more children and young adults survive. A population in which a large number of women are
gainfully occupied will produce more of the things economists

customarily count as income than one in which more women are otherwise engaged. Lengthening of the years devoted to education reduces the number of income-producers, as does early retirement. Incidence of illness or accident affects the time devoted to work.

In the United States the reduction of the death rate at early ages, combined with a falling birth rate (at least until recently), has lessened the proportion of the population composed of children too young to work. More and more women have, on the whole, become income-earners. On the other hand, more years than formerly are devoted to education, and recently more elderly people have retired, and at an earlier age. On the whole, the labor force in the United States has been increasing as a fraction of the population, and is a larger proportion than in most countries. It may be increased by the entrance of still more women into paying occupations, further reduction of disease and accidents, and the employment of more old people as longevity increases. Yet it cannot be indefinitely enlarged.

Another important factor in production is the hours devoted to work by those engaged in it. Hours have been decreasing because of a shorter work week and more holidays. There is no absolute limit to the possible decrease of working time, short of zero, provided the nation can do without the products that might have been turned out in the time lopped off the job. It is unlikely, on the other hand, that the tendency will be reversed and that more time than formerly will be devoted to paid work, except in periods of emergency.

A third factor consists of the stock of tools, machines, buildings, and all the other equipment devoted to economic production. The United States has, of course, a large and growing supply of these "capital goods." There seems to be little reason why they might not be indefinitely increased.

Science and technology have at least an indirect influence on the size of the labor force (through improved health, better

food, and voluntary limitation of the size of families). But
their most direct effect is on the most important factor of all—
what is called "productivity."

Productivity

Productivity is here defined as the amount of output that
can be produced per unit of labor and capital. As long as
productivity increases, the population may enjoy a larger income without augmenting the labor force, or even while decreasing it somewhat. People also can take part of their reward, if they wish, in shorter working hours instead of in
more goods and services, and they have done so.

The unit of labor ordinarily used in reckoning productivity
is the man-hour, that is, a man at work for one hour. Many
studies of the subject have compared the national output only
with the man-hours required to produce it. The National
Bureau of Economic Research has recently made a study of
productivity which includes capital as well as labor. The unit
of capital used is a dollar's worth. Preliminary results of this
study suggest that output in the United States per unit of
combined labor *and* capital has increased about 1.7 per cent
yearly for the past eighty years. This rate is not an entirely
steady one; productivity grows faster in some periods than in
others. Yet on the whole it has shown no tendency to slow
down. Like the increase in per capita income, the increase in
productivity accumulates in the manner of compound interest.
A curve picturing productivity would be an accelerating or
exploding curve. It constitutes, in fact, the main origin of the
exploding curve of per capita income.

The tendency to increasing productivity is widely spread
throughout the economy. Though some industries have registered faster gains than others in output per labor-capital unit,
none yet examined shows a decline. Even in wholesale and

retail trade a gain is observable, though this is not an industry where automatic machines and power have in the past played a leading role.

An old economic doctrine, the so-called "law of diminishing returns," states that in every industry there comes a point where the addition of more labor and capital fails to increase the output. If this happened in industry after industry, and no new industries popped up, the law would apply to the economy as a whole. In that case national productivity would stop rising. It is therefore particularly interesting that the National Bureau study finds no principle of diminishing returns operating in *any* industry.

Some industries, it is true, stagnate and some decline, while others grow. Yet in the industries which have ceased growing, output per labor-capital unit keeps on advancing. The effect of higher productivity is that these industries dispense with labor—their employment declines. Also they may offer less opportunity for investment. (Railroads are an example, as are bituminous coal mines.) But advancing technology takes effect in them as in others.

If all industries were shrinking there would be either heavy unemployment, or a much smaller labor force, or much shorter working hours, but there probably would be no reversal of the tendency of productivity to increase. There was none in the great depression of the 1930s. Productivity did not grow so rapidly as it had in the 1920s, to be sure, but it did grow enough so that although the workers put in a greatly diminished number of man-hours (what with some ten to fifteen million unemployed) and new capital investment almost disappeared, the total national product for the decade as a whole was no smaller than that of the 1920s.

If productivity is doomed to decrease in the future, there is no sign of that event in the past. History points in the other direction.

Technical Progress Cumulates

Because of the picturesque stories about inventors and innovators in the past, it is sometimes difficult to rid oneself
of the impression that technical progress is dependent on the
lucky accident of having a few men with unusually fertile
minds. If at any time we should fail to breed geniuses, progress
might halt. In any event, some suppose science may learn so
much that it will run out of important discoveries; all possible
inventions and improvements may someday be made.

These opinions have been thoroughly discredited by students of the subject. Each scientific discovery creates the possibility of many others. The accumulation of knowledge is a
social process, due to many thinkers and researchers. The
discoverer is simply a man who puts together familiar material
in a new and significant way. The most important discoveries
and inventions come at a time when the pile of knowledge has
grown big enough to make them possible; they are usually
made by several individuals at about the same time. The
growth of each branch of knowledge strengthens every other
branch and increases its potentialities.

There are always new possibilities of discovery. There is always a large amount of new and reliable knowledge which
has not yet been put to any practical use. There are always a
large number of devices in the testing stage, and a large number used by a few concerns but not yet widely adopted. An
improvement in one industry is likely to lead to improvements
in a dozen others. If there is any worker in the field of science,
pure or applied, who thinks that the outer boundary of his
world of learning or of skill is in sight, I have never heard of
him. Nothing appears to limit the growth of knowledge or of
its application but the limited willingness of men to devote
energy to the endeavor.

As long as the interest in discovery survives, or as long as any remain to feel that interest, the sciences and arts which form the basis of modern production are more likely to grow by geometrical progression than to wither away. It is much more difficult to get started at the increase of productivity than to carry it on once a technical civilization has a firm foundation. These are the facts that underlie the accelerating curve of productivity.

Could Power and Materials Give Out?

There may, however, be environmental obstacles to a continuation of the exploding productivity curve. In order to inquire into this matter, let us look at the essence of the process.

Two major lines of parallel development have so far been at work. One is the substitution of inanimate energy for the muscles of men and animals. The other is the substitution of mechanical devices for human skills. Thus the early power loom was at once a machine activated by water power or by steam power instead of by human hands or feet and a device that performed automatically at least some of the operations that previously had depended on the weaver's skill.

There may sometime be an end to the unused sources of inanimate power. The earliest to be employed—wind, falling water, and tides—are apparently self-replenishing. Though they are limited in quantity, the possibility of harnessing them, and of using more and more efficiently the potential energy they offer, is still far from exhausted. The industrial revolution soon added to these the exhaustible resources that can be transformed into usable energy through heat—wood, coal, and later petroleum and natural gas. In highly industrialized regions it is easy to burn wood faster than it can grow. Coal, petroleum, and gas are fossil fuels manufactured by natural processes that require geologic ages; so far as we know they are not now being replenished as rapidly as they are being used up. There are still, however, many unexploited deposits.

Predictions that oil was on the point of exhaustion have again and again been proved false by the discovery of rich new fields. In addition, the efficiency with which these fuels are transformed has grown rapidly and may continue to increase. The world apparently faces no serious shortage of the familiar source of energy for years to come; nevertheless it is unlikely that they could be the basis of anything like an infinite expansion of production.

Harrison Brown, in his recent book *The Challenge of Man's Future*, has brought together several informed estimates, all of which are necessarily uncertain, concerning the future adequacy of energy resources to maintain industrial civilization. In the United States the demand for energy is rapidly increasing—between 1900 and 1950 it grew nearly 20 per cent every ten years, and in the decade 1940–1950, which contained World War II, it increased almost 50 per cent. But on the comparatively moderate assumption that in the future the use of energy in this country will expand 50 per cent every fifty years, Mr. Brown finds that domestic reserves of coal and oil together may last anywhere from seventy-five to two hundred and fifty years. Of course oil, and perhaps eventually coal, will be imported, but other regions will need to conserve their own reserves to support a growing industrialization, and some regions already have a short supply.

Mr. Brown estimates that full development of water power for generation of electricity in the United States—at ordinary minimum flow of the streams—would supply only a little more than 2 per cent of the nation's energy requirements at the present rate of consumption.

Nuclear physics is on the point of conferring on mankind atomic power. This may gradually be substituted for, or added to, other sources of energy. Recent estimates of the quantity of uranium and thorium, the chief fissionable materials, show that these minerals cannot last indefinitely, though their full potentiality is still far from being realized. Probably other substances more plentiful, like ordinary rocks, can eventually yield usable nuclear power. As far as their energy content is concerned, they could fulfill requirements for many thousands, and perhaps millions, of years.

Solar radiation is an enormous source of energy still unused for mechanical purposes. Techniques for collecting it now in prospect might enable one acre of Arizona land, according to Mr. Brown, to provide the energy resources for fifteen persons at the present American level of per capita consumption. The whole present power needs of the United States might be met from the sunlight falling on 50,000 square miles—a tract of 100 by 500 miles. Yet present estimates of the capital cost are relatively high—something like four times the cost of electricity generated from coal.

The best answer to the question whether energy resources, at least on earth, are sufficient to permit unlimited expansion of the technological revolution is probably—No. But the judicious inquirer must at once add that the limit is so far from being in sight, especially if allowance is made for probable further discoveries in the conversion of energy, that any real need for more power may cease before the limit is reached.

Materials out of which industrial products are made may become scarce. Any particular metal or other mineral is limited in quantity and is exhaustible. Yet one cannot foresee the end of the technological revolution merely by predicting the exhaustion of deposits of any few substances, no matter how basic or "strategic." The limit of exhaustion is constantly being pushed further away by reclamation of used materials, as in scrap steel or copper. Substitutes are continually being developed, as aluminum for steel, or magnesium which may be made from sea water, titanium, and other light metals. The efficiency of metals themselves is being improved by better processing and alloying. More plentiful raw materials are being substituted for diminishing ones. Chemical processing makes use of replenishable products which farmers can grow.

As high-grade deposits of iron, copper, and other essential metals grow scarce, lower-grade deposits will be used—at a higher cost in energy. Eventually mankind may depend on grinding up granite and other rocks for his minerals. "The basic raw materials for the industries of the future," Mr. Brown declares, "will be seawater, air, ordinary rock, sedimentary deposits of limestone and phosphate rock, and sunlight. All the ingredients essential to a highly industrialized society are present in the combination of those substances. . . . The industries of the future will be far more complex and highly integrated than those of today. The 'sea industries' will dwarf all existing mining operations."

There are, of course, limits somewhere to useful materials which can be extracted from the earth, or from the seas which beat upon it, or from the air which surrounds it, or from the vegetation which can be grown on its soils or in its waters. But to say that these limits will be approached in a calculable number of years is like saying that man must soon disappear from the earth because in primitive societies the amount of game which he needed as food and the flint which tipped his weapons could not last forever. Tribes have disappeared for such reasons; but man has survived because of his ability to adapt to changing conditions through inventiveness and refusal to surrender. Predictions of doom because of scarce resources usually assume that the technology which determines the use of resources will remain approximately in its existing state. That is a dangerous assumption.

Capital Has Become More Efficient

One important aspect of this subject merits special mention. In a society which increasingly replaces manpower by factories and machines, more and more of the earth's resources must, one would think, be used to make and replace the buildings and equipment themselves. Would not a gigantic industrial plant, which comes so close to automatic production that few workers can be found in it, take a heavier toll of metals from the earth's crust than the few simple tools used by craftsmen of a century ago? In some cases this is doubtless true, but there are countervailing possibilities to be considered. Great advances are being made, not only in the mechanization of production, but in the design and cost of buildings and machines themselves.

An example recently given by the Automobile Manufacturers Association illustrates the point. "In 1912 it took 162 machines to finish the four flat surfaces of 108 cylinder heads an hour. By 1946, the same result was achieved from six machines. Last year [1953] these six machines were replaced by one huge horizontal broach—and from 1912 to 1953 total investment in needed machines dropped from $243,000 to $230,000." Clearly a part of this saving must be attributed to reduction in the metal needed for the machine.

That such examples are typical of what has recently been happening in American industry is indicated by a study made for the National Bureau of Economic Research, *Capital and Output Trends in Manufacturing Industries,* by David Creamer. His findings are that although before 1919 it took an increasing amount of real capital to produce a given output, since that date the amount of real capital needed for the same output has decreased. The adjective "real" indicates that all changes in prices have been accounted for in the calculation. If prices had not risen or fallen at all, plants and machines necessary to the production of the same amount of output would cost less now than in 1919. Mr. Creamer does not analyze in detail why they cost less, but it is extremely likely that one element in the reduction is that less bulky and hence less material-consuming devices are being used per unit of output.

The study begins its analysis with 1880. Ever since then,

productivity has been increasing. In the earlier years the
reason seems to have been that machines, replacing labor,
reduced labor time required for each unit of product. Since
1900 the figures permit a more exact statement. "From 1900
to 1929 the main cause for the reduction in man-hours per
unit of output was the replacement of labor by capital. This
is suggested by the continuous increase in capital, total or
fixed, per man-hour worked. However, between 1929 and
1948 there was a slight decline in the amount of capital provided for each man-hour worked; nonetheless, man-hours per
unit of output continued to decline at a rate comparable to
that of 1900 to 1919. An important cause seems to be the
increased efficiency of capital."

More efficient capital means that more can be produced
with a machine of a given real cost. The real cost of a machine
consists to a considerable extent of the labor and materials
that go into its manufacture. It consists also of the investment
in the machines used to make machines. But if these brood-
mares of the industrial system are also becoming more efficient, we have a pyramiding of efficiency that must mean
widespread conservation not only of human work, but also of
natural energy and natural resources.

Nobody can say whether this trend will continue. It might
be reversed. But since it has happened, it at least can happen
in the future. Western man is not necessarily faced, if he is to
pursue his technological advance, with a gargantuan accumulation of mechanical equipment that will eat him out of house
and home.

Resources Are Ultimately Exhaustible

Neither in the possibility for advance of human knowledge
nor in scarcities of power and materials is there any sure
evidence that the exploding curve of productivity will meet
a decisive check, at least within the next century or so, and at

least in the United States. Yet there are ultimate limits as well as dangers along the way. A highly concentrated and integrated industrial order is highly vulnerable to destruction by modern warfare. And if, for this or any other reason, science and invention should lag, so that new sources of power and new materials should not be developed before old ones give out, technological civilization might collapse without possibility of recovery on the planet earth. For by that time men could not begin all over again to use copper, iron, and other elements which no longer could readily be found in easily usable form. The highly technical laboratories and industrial establishments, once destroyed or fallen into ruin, could never be rebuilt.

Such considerations give rise to the question whether, after all, mankind need always want indefinitely increasing quantities of things. Will populations necessarily keep on growing? Will each member of the population continue to look forward to an ever-expanding quantity of material wealth? Are there not already tendencies in modern society which, even during the next century, and even in the United States, may somewhat limit the demands of the population on the terrestrial globe which sustains it? And in that case, what spurs of necessity, what ambitions and aspirations, could take the place of the motives provided by a materialistic technology, and how would men and women spend their lives? Before proceeding to examine such questions, it is necessary to look into other aspects of the technological society which we know.

3

THE SKILLS OF MACHINES

Near the beginning of the industrial revolution reformers charged that factory operatives were being forced to behave like machines; the complaint has been repeated frequently ever since. Now modern machines, for example, the electronic computer, are behaving more and more like people. This turn of events calls for a fresh look at the long process of mechanization and its effect on persons engaged in production. Although man existed long before machinery, it is impossible in the modern world to understand man without understanding the machines he has made, or to understand machines without understanding the men who made them.

Man making something with his hands has long been impelled to devise implements by which he could do his work better, more easily, or faster. Ancient inventions like the potter's wheel, the primitive hammer and the chisel, the hoe and the shovel, the domesticated fire—such aids to production were servants of the craftsman's purpose. They were extensions of his hands and means by which he could refine his skills. These tools clearly were not masters of those who used them; on the contrary, they enlarged the mastery of the workers. And nothing anti-human seemed to be involved when implements of a somewhat more complex order were developed, such as the spinning wheel and the hand loom.

Division of Labor Broke Up Crafts

It was division of labor rather than machinery as such that gave rise to the charge that the craftsman, who derived creative satisfaction from the fashioning of a whole and meaningful product, was being split into sub-human fragments when he was required to perform over and over again one operation which was only a small part of the work involved in producing the completed object. And division of labor began before machines were much more than simple tools. Adam Smith's famous passage on pin-making illustrates the point. *The Wealth of Nations*, published in 1776, antedated the main mechanical achievements of the industrial revolution even in Britain, where machinery first flourished. In this book Smith wrote: "One man draws out the wire, another straights it, a third cuts it, a fourth points it, a fifth grinds it at the top for receiving the head; to make the head requires two or three distinct operations; to put it on, is a peculiar business, to whiten the pins is another; it is even a trade to put them into the paper; and the important business of making a pin is, in this manner, divided into about eighteen distinct operations. . . ."

A man or woman who spent long days, six or seven days a week, putting heads on pins or sticking them into paper can scarcely have enjoyed much variety or creative satisfaction, even though he used nothing but the simplest of tools in the operation. But this aspect of the matter did not engage Adam Smith's attention. What interested him was that by this means ten persons could make more than 48,000 pins a day or 4800

per man, whereas any one of them by himself could scarcely
have made 20. Thus division of work "increases the productive
powers of labor." It yields more and cheaper things. The critic
of the industrial revolution never questioned this; rather he
asked, "At what human cost?" and "To what end?"

In Adam Smith's view, it was the division of labor which
gave rise to machines, not machines which gave rise to division
of labor. Not only that, but, according to him, "a great part of
the machines made use of in those manufactures in which
labor is most subdivided, were originally the inventions of
common workmen," who made the inventions to obtain
"readier and easier methods" of performing their jobs. A picturesque example is that of the first steam engines, in operating which "a boy was constantly employed to open and shut
alternately the communication between the boiler and the
cylinder, according as the piston either ascended or descended. One of these boys, who loved to play with his companions, observed that, by tying a string from the handle of
the valve which opened this communication to another part
of the machine, the valve would open and shut without his
assistance, and leave him at liberty to divert himself with his
playfellows." This boy apparently exercised no such caution
as an older worker might have felt in inventing himself out of
a job, but both doubtless would have regarded the improvement as a release from tedium and monotony. Imagine eight
boys under the hood of your eight-cylinder car intent on opening and closing its valves, and you will admit that there are
better uses for boys' time, not to speak of more efficient ways
of designing a motor.

Exploitation of Wage-Earners Antedated Machinery

Machinery, then, often tended to relieve monotony and to
release labor for more meaningful occupations. This is not to
say that the employer, in introducing machinery, was moved

by the relief it might offer to the worker. His aim was, at least in the setting of his business, to reduce labor cost per unit of product and so to make more profit.

Low wages and long hours were already common in the early nineteenth century, when industry after industry became mechanized. Yet they constituted an unfortunate aspect of the social order as a whole, including the state of employer-employee relationships and the crude spirit of individualistic enterprise, rather than a consequence of machine production itself.

Indeed, the most moving cases of misery in the working class cited by Karl Marx, the arch-enemy of capitalism, concerned, not industrial machine operators, but exploited craftsmen. In his *Capital* he summarized a news article from a London newspaper of 1863 about one Mary Ann Walkley, a milliner, who worked on the average 16.5 hours a day and in the season 30 hours without a break. On one particular occasion she worked 26.5 hours with sixty other girls, thirty in a room, with insufficient air. She fell ill on Friday and died on Sunday. The physician who attended her testified before the coroner's jury that she "had died from long hours of work in an overcrowded workroom, and a too small and badly ventilated bedroom." The newspaper headline was "Death from Simple Overwork."

Another instance was that of bakers, each of whom performed the complete operation of making and kneading dough, baking loaves and rolls, transporting them to the shop and distributing them in carts—a series of operations that consumed so much time that they had little left for sleep and for which they were paid a pittance. Milliners and bakers—craftsmen indeed, who were not slaves of any machine but would have welcomed an opportunity to delegate more of their work to mechanical devices so that they could have enjoyed at least enough leisure for sleep and earned a living wage, as most modern milliners and bakers do.

Craft-Replacing Machinery

Change, especially great social change, does not take place without discomfort. It may indeed injure many. This was true in the heyday of industrial mechanization, when craftsmen's skills were rapidly being supplanted by machines which could do at least the major part of craftsmen's jobs. The hand spinners and weavers working at home in "cottage industry" were rapidly supplanted by spinning jennies and power looms in textile mills. The spinners' and weavers' crafts became of little use; the sales of their products shrank because the mills flooded the market with cheap goods. The mills in turn used women and children for the simple operations needed in machine-tending; relatively few skilled men were required. The victims exchanged country life for slums, self-directed labor for long hours under supervision, a skilled and usually pleasant occupation for unemployment or monotonous and ill-paid work. Revolt against these evils stimulated the violent outbreaks in which machines were destroyed in Britain and gave rise to the Chartist movement with its demands for labor reforms.

Shoemakers, who had often had trouble with employers before the advent of machinery, lost their old craft and became more than ever dependent on the factory system when modern shoe machinery entered the process. Tailors and seamstresses did not escape exploitation when sewing machines and other mechanical equipment became available to manufacturers, who established a steadily widening market for ready-made clothing.

Machinery, which made possible more production in less time, did lay the basis for shorter hours, higher wages, and better working conditions, which individual workers using the old skills could not attain; yet these benefits were not achieved without long struggle. If they had been, it is probable that the

labor movements which today are strong in every highly industrialized nation would not have been so persistent in the
face of the bitter opposition they once had to face. Even
granted that hours *can* shrink and wages *can* increase when
machines replace craftsmen, the occupation of the machine-
tender repeating the same operation hour after hour seems, at
least to the observer, a poor substitute for the working life of
the creator of a whole product, who has to summon to his
task human faculties which lie dormant in the working hours
of ordinary factory operatives. It may be better to be a well-
protected and fully nourished semi-skilled worker than a
cruelly exploited artisan; but is this the only possible choice?

The kind of machinery characteristic of the industrial revolution up to the end of the nineteenth century was largely intended to substitute mechanical fingers and arms for hand
skills, to replace artisanship by built-in mechanical design.
More and more it did away with skilled hand work, whether
for good or for ill. It even took out of the home many unpaid
jobs formerly done by members of the household, more of
whom now spent their time earning wages from others and
spent their wages buying products that their grandfathers and
grandmothers had made for themselves.

Many suppose that machinery which tended to displace old
skills is the sum and substance of the industrial revolution.
But there are three other main kinds of machinery, embodying
skills different from those of the craft-machines, and these
three other kinds are perhaps even more significant.

Power-Developing Machinery

The first in time consisted of mechanical devices to extract
energy from sources other than the muscles of men and animals, in order that the new machinery might be activated.
Without the power of wind or falling water, even the earliest
mechanized mills or factories would have been impossible. A

most significant difference between the hand loom and the
power loom was that the first was moved by muscle, the second by non-human energy. And when the steam engine was
added to the water wheel, mills and factories no longer had to
be clustered about flowing streams.

Just as important to the development of modern civilization
was the powered transportation which widened markets and
brought access to distant sources of material. Water trading
existed, to be sure, when slaves bent their backs to oars and
donkeys or men pulled river rafts or canal boats. But it was
multiplied by many thousands when sailing vessels could nav-
igate oceans, and later multiplied again when steam power
supplemented sail on the high seas and steam vessels began to
ply the rivers. Land transportation was extremely limited, and
trading consequently narrow, when merchants could not sell
their goods far from the water courses except by caravan, ox
cart, or horse-drawn vehicles plodding over primitive trails.
The steam locomotive and the iron rail changed all this in one
or two generations. Would anyone regret the passing of the
galley slave or deplore unemployment for the camel, the ox,
or the draft horse? The sailors who swarmed up to the yard-
arms practiced an arduous and adventurous art, as did the
driver of the stagecoach or the covered wagon, but aside from
romantic antiquarians few would prefer such a life to that of
the modern seaman or the locomotive engineer.

Energy from coal supplanted energy from wood. Thereafter
conversion of heat energy to electric power by efficient processes has diminished work for the coal miners. Oil pumped
from the earth has done even more to close mines. Too bad for
the miners who lose their jobs, but not many youngsters would
freely choose mining as a life's vocation.

In general, the tapping of non-human energy to push, pull,
and drive has been clear gain for all concerned. A procession
of trailer trucks on a concrete road may be less pleasant to

look at than a wagon train winding across the prairie, but even aesthetically the airplane rivals the clipper ship. Incidentally, growth in the use of mechanical energy has almost exactly paralleled the gain in output per man-hour, and has had much to do with making it possible.

Machinery to Replace the Unskilled

Machinery to replace the skill of craftsmen and machinery to supply motive power still left the "unskilled" in city and country—men who used pick, shovel, and wheelbarrow to dig ditches, make and repair roads, feed furnaces, carry loads, or work the land. They received the lowest wages of all. Their numbers were continually augmented by human fertility or, at least in the United States, by immigration. For decades it seemed scarcely worth while for employers to use machinery to replace them. The costs for depreciation and upkeep of such machinery might easily be greater than the wages paid for muscular work. Also, outside of industrial plants, the unskilled were often used in scattered or remote places to which mechanical power could not readily be conveyed.

Early in the twentieth century all this began to be changed. Universal education prepared people for more remunerative tasks. Beginning with World War I, the stream of immigration dried up. Wages rose, and wages at the bottom rose more than those at the top. At the same time gasoline and Diesel engines made it possible to generate power in small units wherever it might be required. Belt conveyers and automatic stokers in industry, road machines, concrete mixers, bulldozers, tractors, trench diggers, farm machinery adapted to small units of land—these and hundreds of other devices proved efficient substitutes for muscular arms, legs, and backs.

As a consequence the unskilled worker began to disappear. During the steel strike of 1919 I asked an engineer attached to a large steel mill what his attitude was toward the strike. He replied that he was not interested because it was a strike of the unskilled. Shocked by this seeming snobbery, I asked if he did not believe the conditions of the unskilled should be improved. (Many worked a twelve-hour day and seven days a week.) His answer was, "No, we are not going to improve the conditions of the unskilled, we are going to abolish them." Since then his intention has nearly been fulfilled.

In 1910 laborers in city and country comprised 21 per cent of the total labor force; by 1940 they were only 11 per cent. Some will probably always be needed, but even those still classified as laborers usually do their jobs in a very different way from the old "pick-and-shovel" men. Mechanical aids have greatly lightened their load and increased their productivity. Neither the highly skilled nor the laborers have been growing in numbers nearly so rapidly as the semi-skilled operatives and the clerical employees.

Machinery to Operate Machinery

Having encroached on the work both of the skilled craftsman and of the unskilled, technology now goes on to find mechanical substitutes for the semi-skilled machine-tenders and the clerks. This is the culmination of the technological revolution, as far as mechanized production of goods and services is concerned. Not only new machines but whole industrial plants are being designed to embody the new slogan, "automation."

Science, the official organ of the American Association for the Advancement of Science, in its issue for December 25, 1953, summarized in several columns of small type the achievements of the year in engineering and technology. Among these can be found many items like the following (here quoted verbatim):

A program for putting radios, radars, and electric bomb-sights into mechanized production through use of standard-ized parts . . . that can be assembled by machine.

Progress toward entirely push-button factories included an electronic machine controlled by instructions on a magnetic tape, and an automatic eye operating in the infra-red to give a continuous analysis of liquid chemicals.

Electronic machines to handle such clerical work as pro-duction scheduling and supply problems were under develop-ment.

A mathematical model of an electronic computer that re-produces itself was developed.

A new type of "brain" utilized 10,000 tiny ring-shaped magnets woven into a netting of wires to serve as a memory to store 10,000 bits of information in an instant.

The press, both technical and general, is full of bits of infor-mation that show the trend. A milling machine has been in-stalled at the Massachusetts Institute of Technology Servo-mechanisms Laboratory which, guided by a strip of punched tape, can automatically mill a complete machine part. "If the product," writes an author in the *Science Newsletter* of Feb-ruary 7, 1953, "begins to vary from the product 'described' by holes in the tape, the machine makes corrections." This ma-chine can do many types of milling simply by a change of tapes.

In petroleum refineries, writes the same author, special in-struments not only close switches and stop the process the moment anything goes wrong, but insert the proper correc-tions to keep the product up to specifications.

Automobile plants, already highly efficient, have embarked on a major program of automation which will facilitate a bet-ter product at lower cost. This includes not only such relatively familiar things as huge rotary grinding machines, which per-form scores of operations with variations of accuracy kept to ten-thousandths of an inch by electronic rather than by human controls, but even new methods of automatic painting, described as follows by the Automobile Manufacturers Association: "Work to be painted is given an electrostatic charge, while the paint itself is given a charge of the opposite polarity. When released the paint is attracted to the work like a nail to a magnet. Overspray is practically eliminated, water curtains and spray booths no longer needed."

There is almost no limit to the possibility of substituting mechanical means for operations formerly directed by human eyes and executed by human fingers. Putting the material into the machine, starting the machine, stopping it, taking the product out, watching for mistakes or spoiled work, correcting errors, inspecting and discarding, counting, remembering— these are among the kinds of things the new "calculating and control machinery" can do. Go into many a new factory and you will find rooms full of machines pounding and humming away all by themselves, with no human attendants except a few mechanics walking about to keep them in order or to set them for a different operation. In few banks any more will you see bookkeepers bending over ledgers, making entries by hand, or adding and subtracting figures. Tellers still deal with the customers across the counter, but once the deposit is made or the check cashed, the bookkeeping is largely done with cards and automatic machines.

Information and Feedback

Long ago, when crafts were divided into enough separate parts, it became possible to invent devices that would do each part quite passably. The operation was repeated as long as power was channeled to the machine, the machine remained in good working order, and materials, raw or partly finished, were fed into it. What remained for the human operatives to do was to turn the switches or valves, to handle the material before or after the operation or both, to inspect the finished parts, and to assemble them. This sort of thing needed the human eye to watch and discriminate, the human hand to respond to the messages sent by the brain after the eye (or in some cases other sense organs, such as those of touch) had reported to the central nervous system. The machinery was an improvement because it could work faster on the operations for which it was set than could the craftsman. Often, also, it was stronger, and often the quality of its work was as good or even better. It took over the routine and supplied the muscle.

What distinguishes machinery of the new type is that it takes over the responsibility of the eye and the brain. It consists of mechanical devices to *operate* machines—devices often called servomechanisms. Though extremely varied in detail, this machinery makes use of basic principles that physiological psychologists have found helpful in understanding the human nervous system. Names for these principles have become familiar in the language of both engineers and psychologists. One is *information*. Another is the *feedback*. Indeed, it has been suggested that the new control and computing machinery be called *information* machinery as distinguished from the familiar *power* machines.

An illustration of information and feedback is the device familiar to householders who have thermostats on their heating systems. In the good old days the man of the house built a fire in the furnace. If the skins of the family told them it was too hot, he closed dampers; if too cold, he opened dampers or put on more fuel or both. A thermometer in a strategic location helped to settle arguments about how warm it was. It also served to act as a signal—this time conveyed to the brain through the eye—by means of which the operations of the furnace-tender were activated. He was the semi-skilled operator of the machine called the furnace.

Now dampers are opened or closed, coal or oil put into

furnaces or shut off, without the intervention of any human slave of the machine. All the householder does is to set the thermostat at the desired temperature. The thermostat receives from a thermometer the *information* as to whether the temperature is above or below the level set. If above, an electric contact activates a power circuit which shuts off the furnace. If below, another electric contact activates a power circuit which turns it up. This whole process represents a *feedback*. The furnace, by changing the air temperature, feeds information into the thermostat, and the thermostat feeds back to the furnace the command as to what must be done.

Another familiar example of the feedback is the governor on an old-fashioned stationary steam engine, which keeps it going steadily at the desired speed by letting in more steam when the engine lags and partly closing the steam valve when the engine speeds up. Still another, perhaps less familiar, is the automatic helmsman on a modern steamship. The pilot sets the compass course he wishes to take, and a power mechanism moves the rudder accordingly. But waves, winds, and currents may cause the ship to veer off the set course. A feedback device continuously compares the actual direction of the ship with the desired one, and moves the rudder back and forth just enough to compensate for the error caused by forces outside the ship.

The feedback may be a relatively simple device, like the thermal and electrical contacts of the thermostat. It may be somewhat more complex, like the "electric eye" which opens and shuts a gate, when a passenger approaches it in a railroad station, by a combination of a beam of light and an electrical switch which it activates, or like the part of your radio which helps to keep it correctly tuned to your station by measuring the strength of the incoming radio waves. It may consist of almost inconceivably intricate devices, like the combination of radar and calculator that aims an anti-aircraft gun to hit a rapidly moving plane. In this case the radar reports to the servomechanism of the gun where the plane is at every instant, while the mechanism aims the gun enough *ahead* of the plane to hit it by the time the plane meets the projectile. Note that the necessary corrections involve such variables as the speed of the plane, the speed of the projectile, the distance of the plane from the gun, the force of gravity on the projectile, the resistance of the air, the effect of wind in deflecting the projectile, and perhaps other factors as well. All corrections must be performed so quickly that the time they take does not prevent the gun from hitting a fast-flying plane before it gets out of range.

New Machinery and the Nervous System

A man aiming an anti-aircraft gun without such a device would do it much as you would play a garden hose on a dog running across the lawn (provided you had good reason for watering the dog). The hose shoots a stream of water; the marksman sees how close the stream comes to the target, and by a series of approximations and corrections tries to hit it. He makes no mathematical calculations in his mind (at least no conscious ones). By practice he "learns," as we say, to move his arms or hands so as to direct the stream more and more closely on the dog.

This process, one may infer even without knowing much about the physiology of the nervous system, involves a feedback or at least something very like it. Information goes from the eyes to the brain, informing it how close the stream of projectiles comes to the objective; the brain, by commands to the appropriate muscles, strives to bring the shots closer to the target; this series of commands depends on a series of messages from the eye. That this is probably what goes on may be inferred from the fact that the brain does not figure the whole thing out once and for all in a jiffy and then give instructions to the muscles which enable them to hit the bull's-eye at the first try.

Mathematicians, if they have appropriate information about velocities, range, wind, and the like, can calculate how a gun should be aimed. But the process is so intricate and laborious that the plane would be out of sight long before a shot could be fired. Mathematicians, however, can in advance do the thinking to devise a feedback mechanism which, given the necessary information, can almost instantaneously work out the answer; the answer changing from moment to moment, of course, according to the information received. Engineers can construct such a device so cunningly that it not only imitates what the human brain and hand could do in aiming the gun, but improves upon the human gunner in both accuracy and speed.

The same principles are employed in machines used for production rather than destruction. No longer, where these machines are installed, are men or women needed continually to watch, adjust, and manage the operation of the machine while it is at work.

Electric computers, used for many practical purposes aside from the direct control of productive operations, are said to "remember," to "learn," even to "think." A relatively simple one, according to the *New York Times*, recently built by Professor Roger W. Holmes of Mount Holyoke College in his spare time, can inform the operator whether a proposition stated in logical form is true or false, and can reveal conclusions that necessarily follow a certain form of premise. Of course the logical principles used are built into the machine. The seeker after truth converts a proposition to be tested into mathematical (symbolic) form and sets it up on the machine by manipulation of the proper switches and dials. He then can tell in a moment whether the proposition is correct or not because the machine will flash a green light if it is true and a red light if it is false. This relatively elementary device, which cost $120 (aside from the labor of making it), can be used for five variables in as many as nine different relationships.

A machine used by a prominent hosiery mill reports what styles and colors are selling and where, so that more economical use can be made of salesmen. The manufacturer of another computer advertises that by its use any firm can have "the first thing every morning complete facts and figures, analyzed and summarized, on its previous day's performance." The more intricate computers can solve in a few seconds problems in higher mathematics which would take human mathematicians using pencil and paper weeks, months, or years. Some computers can handle large numbers of simultaneous equations or problems in advanced calculus. The Institute for Advanced Study at Princeton has recently completed a machine to calculate the interaction of the many variables that determine the weather, so that forecasts may be made more accurately in a shorter time and for longer periods.

The possibility of making machines to extend human intelligence and effort seems indefinitely large, since the same principles are involved in calculating and control machinery as in the human brain and nervous system. One recent book that describes the similarity, *Doubt and Certainty in Science*, is by a leading British anatomist, J. Z. Young. In both machine and nervous system, information initiates the action process— information being conceived in the living being as interchange by means of coded messages between the organism and its environment, or interchange within the organism. Both organism and machine have feedback systems to guide action. Both depend on memory, which is information in coded form stored up for future use. In machines, information is stored in magnetic circuits, or punched cards or tape, or photographic film. In the brain it is stored, by some process not fully understood, in cells. The human nerves, like the wires of the electronic computer, bear tiny electrical currents that carry coded messages to the central nervous system and coded commands back to the muscles. In both men and machines, the messages received are sorted out at the center and given shape by the "rules" or models stored up in it. These rules may be built into the machine; in the cortex of the human brain they are largely learned from experience. But machines may be made so that they embody much the same capacity to learn.

A man's productive ability differs from that of any single machine yet built largely because of the far broader capacity of his brain and the far greater intricacy of his informational system. The mechanical calculator of the most modern design may have some scores of thousands of valves; there are in the human brain about fifteen thousand million cells. Just as a simple tool is an extension of an arm or hand, so a calculating and control machine is an extension of a brain. No one of these tools or mechanisms can do every sort of thing that either a hand or a brain can do, but there appear to be few specific operations that a humanly invented machine, now in existence or possible, might not do faster or better than a single hand or brain could do them. Indeed some machines can improve on the performance of whole groups of cooperating men.

Naturally it is more difficult to apply informational and control machinery in some processes than in others. According to Richard L. Meier, an expert on the subject who writes in the *Bulletin of the Atomic Scientists,* in the following industries fully automatic facilities are now thought feasible by industrial designers: electric-power generation; telecommunications; liquid fuels; chemicals; cement and bricks; paper products; containers; synthetic fertilizers; fermentation products (beer, antibiotics, etc.); soaps and detergents.

In another group of even larger industries the designers expect the major processes to become fully automatic, though portions of the work may still require manual skills. These are: fibers and textiles; glass and ceramics; iron and steel; nonferrous metallurgy; printing; machine building; processed foods; mining.

Industries which for the present at least will probably continue ordinary mechanization, but still will depend on skilled operators and semi-skilled laborers are: transport; forestry and wood products; garments; shipbuilding.

These three lists might be greatly extended. Future developments may push the third into the second and the second into the first. But they are enough to show that our mechanical culture is in the midst of a startling change.

"Learning," writes Gilbert W. King in the *Scientific American* of September 1952, "is to a large extent the putting of information into a memory and the development of an ability to recognize corrections. Appropriate or even ingenious actions may then be taken on the basis of the learned and stored experiences. Computing machines are capable of these processes."

"We can expect in the future," writes this author, "automatic machines which will make decisions in business and military operations. . . ." [1]

Muscular effort, manual dexterity, even logical thinking and calculating, can be performed better by machines that man has devised or can in the future devise than they can be performed by man unaided by his devices. The implications of this change are so great and reach in so many directions that they demand imaginative exploration. First of all, let us consider what they may do to employment.

---

[1] As a lowly example he imagines "the inventory machines of two large department stores waging a battle for domination of a market. . . . One inventory machine may suspect, from a spurt in the sale of shirts by the store during an ordinarily quiet period, that the competitive store is in short supply of shirts. If it finds that its own store has a large stock of shirts, it will automatically suggest a sales campaign to put the competitor in an embarrassing position."

4

TOO MANY PEOPLE—
OR TOO FEW JOBS?

About the year 1800 the Reverend Thomas Malthus, in his *Essay on the Principles of Population,* observed that human fertility could increase population in a geometrical ratio. At the same time the food supply, though it might be enlarged from time to time by better agriculture, could not be expanded so rapidly as population, and was ultimately limited by the amount of productive land. "I think," he wrote, "I may fairly make two postulates. First, that food is necessary to the existence of man. Secondly, that the passion between the sexes is necessary, and will remain nearly in its present state."

From these postulates Malthus drew the obvious conclusions. "Population can never actually increase beyond the lowest nourishment capable of supporting it. . . . The difficulty must fall somewhere, and must necessarily be severely felt in some or other of the forms of misery, by a large portion of mankind."

In another passage Malthus wrote: "Population invariably increases where the means of subsistence increase, unless prevented by some very powerful and obvious checks. These checks . . . are all resolvable into moral restraint, vice, and misery." Lacking moral restraint, Malthus argued, the three great scourges that hold down population to the numbers that can barely keep alive are famine, pestilence, and war. Needless to say, this Christian clergyman urged moral restraint as the only remedy.

Now, some who look at the marvels of production under modern technology fear that mankind will be able to produce such a super-abundance of goods and services that there will be no employment for most of those seeking work. In the United States a well-fed population—some would say an over-fed population—depends on only about one-seventh of its number to grow its food and fibers. Even these farmers turn out more than can be sold, either at home or abroad, at prices they regard as fair. Malthus would be astounded to learn that in the United States there is a large calling which makes its money teaching people how not to eat too much. Government warehouses are bulging with unsalable wheat, cotton, and other commodities. Young members of farm families stream to cities every year to seek industrial jobs. Meanwhile in the cities machines are replacing unskilled, semi-skilled, and skilled labor alike. Will the time come when a large part of the population no longer can earn a living, not because there is too little food, but because there is too much food and everything else?

Clearly a civilization cannot at the same time have both too little and too much. The Malthusian fear and the fear of mass unemployment resulting from abundance are exact opposites. Where does the truth lie?

Technology Answers Malthus

History, so far as it can be a guide, points to one conclusion. In Western Europe, North America, and other parts of the world which share roughly the same culture—in other words, where the technological revolution has been adopted—population has increased many fold since Malthus wrote, yet the supply of food and other goods has increased far more rapidly. This in spite of frequent and destructive wars. Even persons in the lowest income levels of the industrial population now suffer much less from hunger, are less subject to disease, and have many more possessions than a century and a half ago, when the population was a small fraction of its present size. In large parts of Asia, Africa, and Latin America, on the contrary, where the technological revolution has not flourished, population increase continually strains against the limits of the food supply. Even when war is absent, famine and pestilence perennially limit the growth of population in many "underdeveloped" countries at approximately the misery level.

The technological revolution, then, apparently has reversed the outcome Malthus expected. In the first place, it has enhanced the productive capacity of land and other natural resources, of labor and capital, to a much greater extent and far more rapidly than he dreamed. Yet procreation has not taken advantage of the opportunity to fill the industrialized nations with a horde big enough to eat them barren, like a swarm of grasshoppers. A reduced birth rate is now observed in every region where technological culture has advanced to a high stage. In some nations the fall has gone so far as to cause alarm; the birth rate is so low as to have brought about, or to threaten, not only a stationary but even a declining population. Germany, the Scandinavian countries, Britain, and other nations, far from discouraging population growth, have tried to stimulate it with family allowances or other social-security measures.

A declining size of families has occurred in almost all industrialized regions. It is possible that biological influences are at work; a carefully controlled experiment recently disclosed that rats on a starvation diet were sexually stimulated more frequently and had larger litters than rats on high protein fare. The chances are, however, that the change, as in most situations involving many active forces, cannot be traced to any single "cause." Many circumstances may have contributed. Families now have higher standards by which to judge what is necessary to life. Children do not go to work at such an early age; instead of contributing to their own support, they are costly to parents at least up to fourteen and usually much longer, because of higher educational requirements. The urban family has ceased to be a productive unit in which larger size often means increased welfare. Technology itself has, in industrialized civilizations, provided access to improved means of limiting births without heroic demands on moral restraint, and at the same time it has greatly widened the circumstances under which these means may be afforded and applied. The many medical services now usually involved in child-bearing and child-rearing make it a somewhat formidable undertaking, to be entered into with foresight and planning, rather than casually as an uncontrolled result of daily living. Almost all the evidence points to the validity of a general conclusion: *technological civilization itself limits the birth rate* (at least up to a point) just as surely as it increases goods and services per worker and per member of the population.

Like any social tendency, this one varies in strength from time to time and from place to place. It seems to be less strong in thinly populated regions with plenty of undeveloped resources—as in the United States before 1900. Widespread in-

troduction of new and more convenient contraceptive methods
may at first be accompanied by a fall in the birth rate more
rapid than will be maintained after the use of these methods
becomes stabilized. Lower birth rates occur in a great depression like that of the 1930s; higher birth rates accompany
wars, which lead to early marriages, as in the 1940s and early
1950s. But careful students of the subject do not expect that
such variations will greatly affect the general trend. In the
United States at least, population growth is likely to cease
within a century, and at a level that will not tax the food
supply.

Modern medical and sanitary practices introduced into an
underdeveloped country will often stimulate population
growth (as, for example, in Puerto Rico). They do this not
by increasing the birth rate, which is already high, but by
reducing the death rate. The great triumphs of public-health
measures everywhere have been in the reduction of infant
mortality and of disease in the early years. As time goes on
the health of the middle-aged is improved. All this increases
the life expectancy of a child on the day of its birth (a very
different matter from prolonging the lives of those who have
already reached maturity).

In the industrialized countries the same result has occurred.
But it has been accompanied by other aspects of the technological revolution, which enhanced industrial productivity
and eventually led to fewer births per family. Doubtless this
will also happen in the underdeveloped countries after they
adopt a technological culture. If the inoculation by technology does not "take," and the underdeveloped countries remain underdeveloped, the chances are overwhelming that
they will cease to practice sanitation after the foreign doctors
and nurses leave, and the death rate will rise again. It takes
a rich culture to support modern medicine.

Underdeveloped regions already supporting a dense population may not be able to attain a falling birth rate in time to avert disaster. In the past, the fall of the birth rate in countries experiencing technological advance has lagged behind a falling death rate for a generation or more. It is quite possible that a nation like China already contains more people than could be supported by its existing resources, even at a high level of technological development. The present intensive cultivation of the land in small farms leads to a low output *per person engaged in agriculture,* but as a rule to a high output *per acre.* Collectivization and mechanization of agriculture may not bring larger crops in the aggregate; indeed, they might easily reduce the yield per acre while they increased the output per farm worker. Yet the enlarged population of industrial cities would mean more mouths to be fed, while the high birth rates in the country would prevent any reduction of the rural population. Such dangers must be reckoned with by those responsible for economic policy in Asia and other thickly populated regions.

If existing tendencies continue in the nations already practicing modern technology, there will be little danger of misery arising from a too rapid growth of population in these nations. To be sure, even a stationary population may eventually eat up, burn up, or waste all the resources of a planet limited in size, but that peril now is so far in the future that it need not concern civilized nations at least for another century or so. By that time so many changes will have taken place that precautions we now take to reserve scarce materials, well justified for the proximate future, may seem to our remote descendants much as the foresight of some ancestral troglodyte would seem to us if he had saved up a cache of bear teeth in fear that coming generations might lack ceremonial necklaces to wear in tribal wars.

Will There Be Enough Jobs?

If, in a nation like the United States, too many mouths to feed are not likely to be a problem, will the opposite peril endanger the people? Will automatic factories, mills, mines, warehouses, and the rest leave too few jobs? Look back at the exploding curve in Chapter II, which indicates an accelerating approach toward the production of an infinite amount in no time at all. That limit will of course never be reached, but closer and closer approximation to it might mean that civilization is rapidly nearing a state in which more than enough for everyone can be produced without paid work for more than a few.

Technological unemployment has been feared, and even predicted by responsible thinkers, many times since the start of the industrial revolution. It has occurred in parts of the economy where sudden changes have not been accommodated without the loss of jobs. But it has never occurred in all industries at once or lasted long. Full employment, or nearly full employment, has been the usual condition in the 1950s, after a century and a half of technological development.

The stock answer to the fear of too few jobs is that technology creates new jobs as fast as it abolishes old ones. It introduces new products, makes old ones cheaper or of better quality at the same price. It increases the purchasing power for these products and widens distribution. Demand thus keeps pace with supply, by and large. Indeed, in periods of inflation demand still exceeds supply and thus drives prices up. Purchasers' wants have never yet been satiated, on a national scale, even in the richest country in the world. Give almost any man more money, and he will try to buy more than he has had in the past.

This answer is still good, and shows every sign of being good for years to come. There probably is an upper limit of income beyond which people cannot or will not spend much more for the ordinary products of industry, but it will take many years to raise the mass of the population to that limit. Poverty in the rural Southeast and in other submarginal agricultural regions still presses for a remedy. Families at the lower income levels in cities would look with amazement at anyone who suggested that they are surfeited with goods. Not many even in the middle reaches easily balance their budgets.

Even if people had all they wanted of things they buy as individuals, there are large unsatisfied needs for things and services they buy as taxpayers. Schools and teachers, roads, parking places, social security, recreation facilities, medical services, slum clearance, housing, conservation of natural resources, protection against violence, domestic and foreign, can barely be provided without unbearably high governmental charges against private incomes. There is much to be done before the whole population is so overwhelmed with goods and services that it can no longer use the labor of all who want work and are fit for it. This fact is, at least in principle, a valid answer to those who fear depression if and when the government cuts back expenditures for armament.

Change in Occupations

There must, of course, be changes in the character of employment. Already great changes of this sort have been occurring. So rapid has been the advance of agricultural science and technology that the proportion of the population engaged in farming, which once was over 80 per cent, has shrunk by four-fifths. Even the absolute number of farmers has had a downward tendency, most of the time, for three decades. The proportion engaged in manufacturing, though it fluctuates up and down rather violently between good times and bad, has also had a declining tendency. Even before the era of automation, it showed signs of shrinking absolutely; from now on it is likely, over the decades, to decline. The same may be said of mining. Fewer and fewer are needed to fabricate the goods for our growing, high-consumption population.

Services and professions, on the contrary, have been in greater demand. Distribution, including wholesaling and retailing, the servicing and repair of automobiles and other mechanical devices, the amusement and recreation trades, teaching, medical service, and a host of other occupations not primarily concerned with making material goods, have expanded more rapidly than the ranks of those engaged in the literal production of goods have shrunk. A sizable and increasing proportion of these services are provided by federal, state, and local governments.

Automation is at work in these fields too. It is sure to make heavy inroads on the routine clerical work of offices, and on retail sales personnel—indeed, it has already done so. Little by little it is eating into the more repetitive operations everywhere. What kinds of work will it leave?

Even in agriculture, manufacture, and mining it will leave the work of designing, planning, directing, managing, dealing with personal contacts of all kinds. It will leave functions connected with diagnosing imperfect performance of even the most advanced machines, repairing them, renewing and improving them. It will leave, as in scientific discovery, technological research, teaching, governmental administration, and health services, work that requires dealing with intangibles, confronting variety and the unexpected. In short, the exercise of trained imagination and other creative faculties which more completely distinguish what we like to think peculiarly human from what we are accustomed to think machine-like will always require the effort of human beings.

If then, as some believe, the human race will always breed a large proportion of dullards, incapable of anything beyond heavy physical labor or indoctrinated routine, there are certain to be millions unemployed because they will be unemployable. But if, as the humanistic tradition and the American faith hold, human beings are capable, through conditioning and education, of much greater achievements than their past environments have trained them for, almost everyone may become qualified to perform the newer kinds of work for which there is now, and will long continue to be, greater demand than formerly.

Gains in Time

So far in this book the story of the gains from technology has only partly been indicated, and perhaps the most significant part remains. Modern civilization has indeed been enabled to support larger numbers, and to support them at higher living levels, by virtue of the production of a steadily growing output per man-hour. But in addition it has immensely decreased the man-hours of work per man and per unit of the population.

Since the early days of the industrial revolution in the United States the following gains have been made in *time*— that is, the time not required to be spent at occupations commonly called "work."

The average work week has been reduced from 60 or even 72 hours to 40 or less.

The average school-leaving age has been advanced from 10 or less to 14 or more.

Paid vacations have become the rule rather than the exception.

Many may, if they wish, retire with an assured income at the age of 65 or thereabouts. (Unfortunately many who do not wish to retire are forced to do so.)

Fully half of the household work formerly done by women in the home has been removed. Many women, to be sure, have followed this work into the factories, offices, stores, and restaurants, but many have not.

Just to illustrate the tremendous gain in human time which this development represents, let us make an exceedingly rough calculation. The present labor force in the United States approximates 65 million persons. Assume that on the average, in a year of relatively full employment, these persons could in a year work 48 weeks of 40 hours each. Multiply 48 by 40 and you get 1920 hours a year per person. Multiply that by 65 million, and you get 124.8 billion hours a year on the job for the whole working force. Now assume that shorter hours had not been achieved, and this same force worked half again as long as it did (60 is 150 per cent of 40). In other words, it has gained, in leisure time, 62.4 billion hours a year. Add 120 hours a year per person to account for paid vacations (2 weeks at 60 hours), and you get an additional time-saving of 7.8 billion hours. Add the time saved from work by all children in school who would have been at work under the conditions of a century or more ago, the time saved from work by the retired, the time saved from household work by women, and you might easily have a total that approximates 100 billion hours a year. This figure is 25 or 30 times greater than the estimated age (in years) of the planet Earth.

If the labor force had not wrested this spare time from the ability to produce more per hour, they would be producing every year at least half again as much as they do, and would have been that much better off in creature comforts. The average family income in the United States would now approximate $7500 instead of $5000. If the gain in real income continues for another eighty years as it has for the last eighty, the average family income at the end of the period, instead of being $25,000, would be $37,500.

Workers have preferred to take a large part of the gain from rising productivity in shorter hours for all who work, and in exemption of more people from work, rather than in a more rapid rise of material welfare than has occurred. The gain was, for many years, bitterly fought for by the wage-earners, and was won only in the teeth of sturdy opposition by employers. Gains in shorter hours have been gradual, though somewhat spasmodic. The most striking have occurred since 1914.

This tendency, too, is likely to continue. As long as the labor supply is adequate, employers have become perfectly willing to insure long enough operation of expensive capital equipment by utilizing three shifts instead of two, and occasionally four shifts instead of three. Workers who can earn enough in shorter periods are likely to want to continue their gains of leisure. One almost certain outcome of the accelerated substitution of machines for human labor will be still shorter hours, longer vacations, more years spent in education, perhaps even more and earlier retirement.

Adjustment Will Be Gradual

The peril of mass unemployment through satiation of wants has been oversimplified and overdramatized by many who have feared it. The picture in their minds seems to be that of a sudden crisis brought about in some particular future year by the collision of satiety with the need for paid jobs.

On Thursday morning, let us say, July 26, A. D. 2030, everyone will wake up with no more desire for anything that can be bought, except to replenish the worn-out articles he already owns. On that same day there will be several million young people added to the labor supply and looking for their first jobs. They will greatly outnumber those already on jobs who on that day are taken ill, die, or retire. Consequently there will never be anything for the extra ones to do, except by displacing a worker who does not want to quit. In addition the millions who have been needed to make not replacements but additional supplies will no longer be able to find work. From that point on, the haggard ranks of the unemployed will also be augmented by the jobless displaced by new and more productive machinery. Society will either have to support a continually enlarging horde of mendicants, or face a revolution. In the end the few technicians and managers needed to operate the factories will be forced, behind their fortified or within their underground work places, to hold off the assaults of a starving population that has no money to buy what the technicians exist to make and the unemployed are no longer needed to produce!

This nightmare is as fantastic in reality as it is in logic. Its crucial flaw is that satiety does not overwhelm people all of a sudden; satiety is a piecemeal and gradual process, and social adjustment to it therefore can be, and has been, piecemeal and gradual.

What has been happening before our very eyes and can be read in all the reliable statistics is that, in the United States at least, a population of a given size has long been getting enough of certain commodities—cyclical depressions excluded. The market for food has reached the point where, by and large, it cannot increase except as the population increases. The same is true of men's shoes. Clothing, rugs and carpets, and other textiles are pressing against the same limitation. Food and clothing are two of three major necessities usually mentioned as basic. The third, shelter, is still in short supply; years of building will be required to satisfy existing needs, but is it not possible to believe that someday everyone will have a dwelling suited to his wants?

Automobiles have several times approached saturation of the market created by those who can afford them, as have other durable goods such as radio and television sets. As incomes rise, the time is sure to come when only replacements will be needed. The market is still active and growing for many other things with which people occupy their spare time—motorboats, sporting equipment, gardening supplies, even reading matter of one kind or another. But even if eventually everyone enjoyed a continual vacation, and indulged as many interests as a human mind can hold, the sale of such articles would still be limited at some point by the time available to use them.

People, one may suppose, will still need sleep, and some time for eating, even at the utmost reaches of technological advance. Can we imagine a whole population spending twelve or thirteen hours a day before their television sets? Perhaps, but in that case there would be no further market for cars, golf clubs, fishing rods, or cellar work benches. Somewhere there is a point of utmost satiety for the things that can possibly be offered for sale.

Yet this satiety, though eventually it may include all commercial articles, develops gradually, product by product, and those engaged in furnishing the particular products are able to make the appropriate changes over a long period of years. Surplus agricultural populations drift to cities, workers in one manufacturing industry contract in number while those in another increase, more young people choose careers in services, professions, government employment, instead of making goods. Partly because of their tradition and partly because of facilities for transportation and communication available nowhere else in such profusion, Americans have an unprecedented mobility. And because of universal educational facilities and relative lack of hereditary stratification of social classes, new generations can adjust themselves to new labor requirements. Dominant in the adjustments, and becoming more dominant as the years pass, is the citizens' choice of more time off the job rather than more things made and earned on the job.

Satiety in practice is after all a relative matter. It seldom presents itself to the consumer merely as the question, "Don't you have enough of this?" but rather, "Wouldn't you prefer more of that?" A well-fed person *can* stuff himself to immobility, but most of us rise from the table when we feel we have had enough, to do other things.

It is true that industrial workers often put in overtime for the extra pay that it brings, but they would not like it as a permanent practice. It is true that when they ask for shorter hours they usually expect the employer to boost the hourly or piece rate so that they will receive as much as before. Yet they know well enough when they struggle for a shorter work week that they are sacrificing potential take-home pay in exchange for the extra time they win for themselves. People who live quite modestly frequently prefer less rapid advance in the number of things they can buy in order to enjoy the luxury of being their own bosses for longer periods.

As the number of available things one can buy increases, so does the demand for more time not engaged in making things increase. As satiety of the comparative sort extends over a larger area of commodities and approaches complete satiety for things, so grows the eagerness to be off the job for longer periods. More and more, workers will reward themselves with time rather than with extra goods, as technology piles up the possible profusion of goods by demanding less working time to make a given number of units. Technological unemployment is thus transmuted into technological leisure. This is the ultimate reason why there need be no fear of mass unemployment as a result of automation.

How things will be arranged to give everyone both leisure and income we can only guess; doubtless the problem will be worked out year by year and in detail, with different devices for different situations. In some occupations people may work, say, three days a week for six or even four hours a day, while other shifts take over for the remainder of the time. In other callings yearly vacations may stretch to two months, three months, six months, or more. Funds now devoted to pensions, unemployment compensation, and the like, and invested in corporate securities, may ultimately be used to add capital income to earned wages. One thing is certain: more young people will spend more years on their education. More older people, too, may go back to school, not merely to prepare for advancement in vocations, but to explore the boundless realms of the mind and the arts. Millions would now do so by choice if there were room for them in the educational institutions and if they could earn enough in the time left from studies to pay the necessary costs.

No problem of technological unemployment can possibly accompany the utmost reaches of the technological revolution if most people can be fitted to do the kinds of jobs that will be left to do. The adjustments may not be easy; rapid change will, as always, be uncomfortable. Some are bound to suffer in the process. In particular, the nation cannot afford to allow the change to be complicated by the mass unemployment, not technological in origin, that accompanies a severe depression. No inevitable fate, however, will compel many to go for long without remunerative work, so long as the American economy and the American labor force remain as flexible as they have been in the past, and so long as progressing satiety can be offset by progressing avidity for time to do things for which money rewards are not offered.

The ultimate gain will, of course, be more time under the command of individual persons. The changes in Western cultures that this gain may involve are those which are of overwhelming importance. What would a civilization be like in which most of the adult population is no longer at work earning a "living" most of the time?

5

IS THE GAME WORTH THE CANDLE?

The industrial-technological revolution, under the aegis of what is roughly called capitalism, has never been whole-heartedly accepted either by a majority of the human race or by many of the most powerful or sensitive thinkers in the regions where it has thrived. It is today loudly acclaimed in the United States as the ultimate achievement of democracy and liberty. Expressions of dissent have fallen to ebb tide, mainly because of hostility to the chief force which now challenges it—Russian-Soviet power. But internal opposition either to the regime of capitalist industrialism as a whole or to various practices associated with it arose early in its course and periodically has been renewed. If ever the tension of outside peril is released, expressions of dissatisfaction will doubtless be heard in the land again.

Marx's Mistaken Predictions

Strangely enough, the opponent of capitalism who has attracted the largest number of professed followers, Karl Marx, is the easiest to refute on the basis of the record. As industrialism developed, he predicted, workers would suffer increasing misery. They would be kept—as Malthus and Ricardo, both in the classical capitalist tradition, had argued—at a level of mere subsistence. Employers would use technical advances, not to reduce hours or increase wages, but to enlarge their profits and so to accumulate capital. Soon they would produce more than the domestic working population could consume and would be forced to exploit colonial markets, thus making inevitable financial imperialism and war among imperialist nations. Whenever markets gave out, crises of unemployment would ensue.

Agriculture would become consolidated under a few owners; industry would be monopolized. The majority of the population would become a propertyless proletariat, which would in the end, when capitalism collapsed because of lack of markets, revolt against its oppressors and seize the instruments of production.

On almost every one of these counts the reverse of Marx's predictions is now evident. Levels of living of industrial workers have greatly risen. Hours of work have been much shortened. The distribution of income, according to the best statistical measures, has become less unequal than formerly, at least in the United States and Britain, the two leading industrial nations. Agriculture has not fallen prey to capitalist exploitation. Although industrial corporations have become large, they still compete for the consumers' dollars, and share their gains with their employees. There are still many independent businessmen.

European colonial empires are disintegrating. The largest

profits are made, not in exploiting backward peoples, but in selling to the domestic populations of the industrialized nations themselves. In the United States at least, relatively little private capital is available for investment abroad—less, indeed, than those who desire to advance the welfare of the underdeveloped nations wish its owners would risk.

Most striking of all, the industrial proletariat as Marx conceived it has, by virtue of greatly improved technology, a shrinking rather than a growing tendency, and now constitutes a minority of the population in the most advanced industrial states. By virtue of automation, it seems to be on the way toward extinction. In no modern industrialized nation has a Marxist revolution occurred either by uprising or by use of the ballot on the part of the proletariat. So-called Communist overturns have in almost every instance, beginning with Russia, taken place in nations where industry had made relatively little progress. The bulk of revolutionary support has come from agricultural workers in revolt against a feudalistic system of land holding. The possible exception is Czechoslovakia, but there contiguity, Soviet military power, and intrigue played a large role. Certainly spontaneous uprising of an oppressed proletariat can hardly be credited for the changes of regime.

Seldom has a major leader of thought achieved so huge a success in attracting followers, not merely in his lifetime but for generations thereafter, accompanied by such colossal failure in his analysis of events. One cannot dismiss Marxism as a creed and a movement just because Marx's logic was faulty. People must have had some strong impulse to accept it and to follow what they were informed was his program.

Why People Followed Marx

The story, of course, is not told by comparing what Marx wrote in the middle years of the nineteenth century with the situation a hundred years later. His success was in large part derived from the fact that he gave impressive voice to resentment that many felt at the time and have felt, in various places, and on various occasions, ever since. Regardless of the validity of his logic and the truth of his observation, millions have been hostile to industrial capitalism, and of these many have followed leaders who carried the banner of Marxism, though millions have not.

Marx painted a reasonably good picture of what had been occurring when he wrote. The factory system was depriving many individual craftsmen of their livelihoods, and the hours, wages, and living conditions of workers in the factories were indeed miserable. New concerns did not find it easy to obtain outside capital, since the principle of limited liability had not yet been legally granted to joint-stock corporations. Therefore employers had to accumulate funds for expansion out of their profits, and did so as much as possible at the expense of wage-earners. The domestic population in Britain could not buy all that mushrooming industry could produce, and so foreign markets were eagerly sought. Wars of imperialist character had indeed been fought—though more often when merchant capitalists dominated national policy than after the early years of nineteenth-century industrialism. Whenever depression and unemployment arrived, employers were the first to attribute it to "overproduction" and lack of markets. Many socialists who preceded Marx—for example, the British textile manufacturer Robert Owen—had declared that the workers could not buy all that they produced.

Strikes and attempts to organize trade unions were severely repressed, in Britain up to the middle of the nineteenth century, and in the United States during almost all of it. Opposition to labor movements came not merely from employers but from judges and legislatures. In Britain even the franchise was at first severely restricted. Marx's phrase that the state was the "executive committee of the ruling class" was no libel in matters which concerned the condition of the workers and industrial relations.

Non-Marxist Reformers

The continual conflicts between "capital" and "labor," the political attacks on industrialists, the protests of intellectuals with democratic leanings, give evidence that all were not well satisfied with the progress of technology under capitalism. In Britain social change to moderate the rigors of the system began early in the 1800s. Manufacturers in their own interest as well as in that of the workers brought about the repeal of the Corn Laws, which through protection of domestic agriculture raised the price of food to the worker, and in periods of unfavorable weather in England and Ireland even led to famine. Reformers improved working conditions by the factory acts and extended the franchise. Little by little organized labor established itself and won concessions.

In the United States the Jackson era was marked by the organization of unions and by agitation on the part both of labor leaders and of intellectual reformers. Their proposals ranged over the whole gamut of utopian proposals, from shorter hours and universal free education to new monetary schemes, abolition of inheritance, universal free distribution of land, and a new society based upon cooperative producing units to replace private industry. Some of the reforms were carried out little by little; others were tried and failed. None, however, stemmed from Marx's formulations, since at the time he had written no part of his definitive work. In America he was known, if at all, only as an author of the *Communist Manifesto* of 1848 and, somewhat later, as a European correspondent for Horace Greeley's New York *Tribune.*

After the American Civil War the industrial revolution really blossomed in the United States. The history of the latter part of the century is checkered with conflicts relating to control of the American economy by capitalist interests. They centered, not on socialist theory, but on practical affairs like monetary policy, railroads, protective tariffs, combinations and monopolies, low wages, long hours, political corruption stemming from the influence of wealth seeking favors from government. In spite of the fact that industry was rapidly expanding and technological improvement was—aside from depressions—enlarging the material means of life for almost everyone, many farmers and industrial workers were unhappy about the distribution of the gains, and their discontent was shared by enough others so that various rivals of the ruling Republican party, which became identified as the party of business, often threatened its supremacy and won numerous victories, such as tariff reduction, railroad regulation, and antitrust legislation.

After 1900, when the giant industrial consolidations were establishing themselves, there was a veritable outburst of attacks on the ruling interests. This time the reformers were not agitating for utopias; they were pointing out by means of careful research and documentation the sins against democracy, justice, and humanity that had grown up during the wild scramble for wealth. Writers like Ida Tarbell, Lincoln Steffens, Ray Stannard Baker, Upton Sinclair, Burton J. Hendrick, and others wrote about the current abuses for magazines with wide circulation. In the words of the careful historian Harold U. Faulkner, in his *Decline of Laissez Faire*, they "probed into almost every phase of American civilization of the period—corruption in state and national politics, big business, child labor, vice, religion, the press, fake advertising, impure food and drugs. . . . Filled as the articles were with apparently libellous material, no major suit was ever sustained against author or publisher."

Following this wave of protest, the reform administrations of Theodore Roosevelt and Woodrow Wilson reflected the popular desire for curbing those whom Roosevelt had termed "malefactors of great wealth." Railroad regulation and anti-trust legislation were strengthened, banking was reorganized and placed under federal control, and a host of minor regulatory measures were passed. World War I and the Republican administrations that succeeded it marked a period of quiescence for reform, but the financial scandals of the later 1920s and the dramatic collapse into the great depression led to another, and this time an even wider, flowering of legislative remedies and changes.

Who knows but what Marx's predictions would have been verified by history even in the United States if his "capitalist ruling class" had remained unaffected by those who suffered from or disliked its unrestricted operations? Hardly any of these objectors were followers of Marxist doctrine; only a few were even socialists of a milder temper. True, many of the financial and industrial potentates under attack had, all the time, been organizing and releasing the upsurge of more efficient production, which in the end has made possible a better life for all. If it were not for this, revolution might indeed have broken out. Not many of those who tried by monopolistic or other means to restrict wide distribution of the benefits of technology were long successful.

But the process of arriving where we are today was not entirely as easy and pleasant as a statistical summation of the results might imply. Credit for those results must be assigned not merely to the organizers of industrial production and technological improvement, but to the long and varied line of those who fought, often with hazy vision, for the preservation or perfection of democratic and humanitarian aims. It is this whole tradition, not merely that of "private enterprise" in business, which has brought to pass whatever it is that America now has to offer the world.

Marx has not won his great bodies of followers where democracy and industrialism have been able to maintain a

viable though not always happy marriage. Among industrialized nations, Soviet communism found its greatest support
after World War II in France, still suffering from the shock
of defeat and occupation by the Germans and from an inflation which left most wage-earners below their prewar level
of living; and in Italy, where political troubles were com-
pounded by the remnants of a feudal land system, poverty
of natural resources, and overpopulation.

Marx's opposition to capitalism was stated entirely in material terms. The particular social conflicts which have rarely
been absent from the development of the capitalist order have
usually concerned issues also stated in material terms, whether
or not those in opposition were doctrinaire Marxists—and in
the United States usually they were not. It is in these same
terms that the historical answer to Marx lies. Things have
turned out much better than he expected, and in consequence
most people in advanced industrial nations have not been so
dissatisfied as to wish to overthrow the system.

Non-Material Discontents Not Yet Allayed

Another long category of objectors not subject to the creed
or tight disciplinary organization of Marxist parties placed
their emphasis on other considerations. Man does need bread,
clothing, and shelter, but he needs emotional welfare too, and
sometimes prefers a moderate poverty in things to material
riches corrupted by poverty in less tangible satisfactions. This
is an ancient and continually recurring theme of the prophets,
the poets, and the philosophers. It evokes a powerful echo
in almost everyone, provided he has the time and the impulse
to reflect. What is the impact of capitalist industrialism on
intangible satisfactions? The malaise which is often felt in
modern Western culture has had many spokesmen. This type
of objection cannot be answered by statistics about wages,

production, and employment; and no convincing answer to
it has ever yet been made.

Capitalism undermined the medieval feudal order even
before the advent of modern industrialism; the factory system under laissez-faire only struck the final blow. Feudalism
was repressive and unjust in many of its aspects, but, influenced as it was by Christian attempts to spiritualize its
mores, it expressed many values which were missed in its
passing. Capitalist theory, like capitalist practice, placed major
emphasis on the growth of material wealth, and it looked upon
material self-seeking by competitive individuals as the best
means of achieving that end. To many, this emphasis seemed
calculated to wreck the best in mankind. Some wanted to
return to the feudal order; others to supplement the new with
the best of the old.

Adam Smith had written in the *Wealth of Nations* (1776)
that the profit-seeking businessman "intends only his own
gain, and he is in this, as in many other cases, led by an in-
visible hand to promote an end which is no part of his intention. . . . By pursuing his own interest he frequently pro-
motes that of society more effectually than when he really
intends to promote it." In arguing against regulations and interference by the state or other outside authorities Smith
said: "All systems either of preference or of restraint being
taken away, the obvious and simple system of natural liberty
establishes itself of its own accord." This doctrine did not
appeal to those who distrusted unleashed self-interest, and
who were not so optimistic about "natural liberty."

Early socialists who followed the French Revolution believed in the liberation of man but were revolted by the apparently anti-social doctrine of competitive laissez-faire. Louis
Blanc (1811–1882) voiced their dissent by declaring that the
opportunity for human development was frustrated by this
"war of all against all." Comte Henri de Saint-Simon (1760–
1825) attained great influence by his writings. The Church

had lost the spiritual authority it had held under feudalism but, he argued in *The New Christianity*, something was
needed to replace it. Science and technology were indeed the
basis of the new order, but they should not be accompanied
by anarchic individualism and international war. "In the New
Christianity, all morality will be derived immediately from
this principle: men ought to regard each other as brothers."
Hence, he argued, there should be a European government,
with a parliament which the wise and the just would control.
This government, inspired by both science and Christianity,
would install public ownership of industry—so Saint-Simon
believed.

Simonde de Sismondi, a Swiss descended from an Italian
noble family, published in 1819 a work, *New Principles of
Political Economy*, in which he protested, not against private
ownership of wealth as such, but against the ideas of laissez-
faire promulgated by Adam Smith and his followers. He did
not believe that the criterion of values should be wholly material. "Wealth," he wrote, "is a modification of the state of
man; it is only by referring to man that we can form a clear
idea of it." Both moral and physical enjoyment constitute
wealth. Sismondi raised the question whether under the new
capitalist order "man himself belongs to wealth, or wealth
belongs to man." The dignity and the autonomy of man, outside his money-making relationships, seemed to be disintegrating.

A German writer, born just after Sismondi (1773–1842),
expressed another view on much the same subject. Adam
Müller (1779–1829) was concerned about the wholeness of
life, and about the wholeness of the community. Non-profit-
seeking occupations like art, religion, and the services of the
statesman were just as productive, he maintained, as the
making of material goods. Even in the provision of the material necessities of life, the separation of the ownership of
tools from the worker who used them created conflict be-

tween the employer and those whom he hired. The factors of
production were not merely land, labor, and capital, as the
classical economists declared, but also "spiritual capital."
Müller asserted: "The spirit reacts unceasingly against the
division and mechanization of labor, which Adam Smith
prized so highly; the spirit wants to preserve man's personality." Also: "If we say a thing is useful, we mean that it has
value in relation to civil society."

Müller wanted to return, not exactly to feudalism, but to a
similar type of order which would unite people organically.
Later he served Metternich as a protector of the past against
the new atomization of the European social body and of the
individual. The appeal in this type of thinking was later used
by the Nazis as a rationalization of their program, though the
real drive of the so-called National Socialists was toward the
supremacy of the "leader" internally and military conquest in
behalf of a supposed super-race. In action they emphasized
the nationalism and almost ignored the socialism. But, after
all, they embodied in part a powerful, and for a time almost
successful, protest against laissez-faire capitalism, a protest
which has been felt by many who were horrified by their
program and their actions, or would have been horrified by it
had they lived in the 1930s and 1940s.

William Morris, the British poet and craftsman, who was
born in 1834 and lived through most of the rest of the nineteenth century, also felt a lack of values in the capitalist industrialism of his day, values which apparently had been
present in medieval times. Morris had been trained as an
architect and for a time tried painting. It was the aesthetic
poverty of an industrial and commercial regime which revolted him. He founded a manufacturing business which attempted to improve decorative design, and in his Kelmscott
Press did beautiful printing. But he was deeply disturbed
because he could sell his products only to a rich minority.

Also, he knew that the profound satisfaction he derived from his own work as a craftsman could not be shared by those operatives in industry who did not design what they made and who regarded their work as tiresome drudgery. He thought that if inequalities could be leveled, craftsmanship could be restored to its true place; people would make things because they found them satisfying and useful rather than just for the profit of another. Machinery, to be sure, had its uses, but it should be employed to make work easier rather than for individual profit.

Morris's views were shared, in one form or another, by many thinkers who felt ill at ease amid the vulgarities of the Victorian Age. John Ruskin in part gave them expression; Thomas Carlyle denounced the loss of manhood and the nobler qualities of leadership in the commercial melee. The leading and most widely respected economist of the day, John Stuart Mill (1806–1873), in Book Four of his immensely successful *Principles of Political Economy*, published in 1848 (the same year as the *Communist Manifesto*), expressed his moral and aesthetic distaste for the existing society. "I confess I am not charmed," he wrote, "with the ideal of life held out by those who think that the normal state of human beings is that of struggling to get on; that the trampling, crushing, elbowing, and treading on each other's heels, which form the existing type of social life, are the most desirable lot of human kind, or anything but the disagreeable symptoms of one of the phases of industrial progress."

In the United States, Mill observed, where Americans were blessed with plenty of land and little poverty, where democracy and political rights were secure (except for women and Negroes), "all that these advantages seem to have yet done for them . . . is that the life of the whole of one sex is devoted to dollar-hunting, and of the other to breeding dollar hunters. This is not a kind of social perfection which philanthropists to come will feel any very eager desire to assist in realizing."

"Those who do not accept the present very early stage of human improvement as its ultimate type," he went on, "may be excused for being comparatively indifferent to the kind of economical progress which excites the congratulations of ordinary politicians; the mere increase of production and accumulation." Mill looked forward to a state where there could be a better distribution of income and "a much larger body of persons than at present, not only exempt from the coarser toils, but with sufficient leisure, both physical and mental, from mechanical details, to cultivate freely the graces of life."

John Stuart Mill looked in the end for a goal very different from that held up by those who envisioned indefinite "progress" in material wealth and population. "A population," he wrote, "may be too crowded, though all be amply supplied with food and raiment. It is not good for a man to be kept perforce at all times in the presence of his species." This argument he reinforced with a theme that often recurred among those British writers who resented the ugly scars made by modern industrialism on their countryside. "Solitude in the presence of natural beauty and grandeur, is the cradle of thoughts and aspirations which are not only good for the individual, but which society could ill do without. Nor is there much satisfaction in contemplating the world with nothing left to the spontaneous activity of nature; with every rood of land brought into cultivation, which is capable of growing food for human beings; every flowery waste or natural pasture plowed up, all quadrupeds or birds which are not domesticated for man's use exterminated as his rivals for food, every hedgerow or superfluous tree rooted out, and scarcely a place left where a wild shrub or flower could grow without being eradicated as a weed in the name of improved agriculture."

Doors to Escape

The return to nature, also expressed in William Words-worth's famous sonnet beginning:

> The world is too much with us; late and soon,
> Getting and spending, we lay waste our powers,

not only signified a romantic love for trees, birds, and flowers; it was even more a symbol of reaction from the values of industrialism and a commercialized civilization. No better example of this reaction exists than that of Henry David Thoreau, whose *Walden* (1854) is more familiar to literate Americans—as well as to many British and other readers—a century after he wrote it than it was when it first appeared. Thoreau used to be called "naturalist" and "individualist," but now his lasting significance is seen in his revolt against commercial, urban civilization and its values, expressed not socially as in revolution, but in personal withdrawal, to preserve what seemed essential to him. Thoreau could not remain in isolation; physically he soon returned from Walden Pond to the society he deplored, but he lived in it grudgingly, paying to it what tribute one must pay to an alien conqueror, but never surrendering his inner protest. In it, he felt, one must give too much for what one receives in return. What he had to sacrifice was what means most to man; what he received in exchange was necessary, to be sure, but paltry in ultimate value.

"Instead of noblemen," wrote Thoreau, "let us have noble villages of men." And again: "It is not necessary that a man should earn his living by the sweat of his brow, unless he sweats easier than I do." His injunction was: "Simplify, simplify!" Men, he complained, "have become tools of their tools."

The theme of escape has again and again appealed to cultivated Americans, especially when the stirring of hope for something better seemed frustrated by the temporary eclipse of cultural light or lack of real change in the values of industrial capitalism. In the vulgar air of the 1920s, dissenters read with avidity the disillusioned life report of a prominent American, *The Education of Henry Adams*. Many saw in medieval cathedrals the surviving expression of beauty in living and in art which the modern world—especially the American world—had lost. Though at the time most young Americans thought Henry James snobbish, they were aware of the freedom to write and live as an honest creator which he had achieved by escape to Europe. Young poets, novelists, and critics themselves became émigrés, and it was largely from these that the lasting contributions of the period to American literature eventually came.

Unlike Henry James, many of those who in the 1920s fled to the Left Bank of the Seine had no private fortunes to sustain them while they wrote and lived as they pleased. It was not merely the stale mental atmosphere of the United States which stifled them, but the obvious material fact that they could not find time to write what Americans probably would not buy in sufficient quantities to keep them alive, as long as they held jobs which would enable them to eat and clothe themselves while they tried to write. On the other hand, because of what solemn British economists called the "undervaluation of the franc," they learned that a few dollars would go a long way in the very place where they found a more appreciative audience and more stimulating companions.

The trouble was not that in the United States many were getting richer, or that technical progress, which seldom moved faster than in the early 1920s, was itself evil. Few poets or artists would have rejected financial success if it had come to them. Objectors were not disposed to choose between two completely different worlds, in one of which puritanical simplicity would be accompanied by justice, beauty, and truth, and in the other of which luxury and ease would betray the human spirit into obliquity and stupidity. The trouble was that what one had to do in order to acquire one's share of prosperity left no room for the independent pursuit of what one believed had real value.

For every émigré, there were thousands of good Americans who stayed at home, working at their accustomed pursuits and thinking their own thoughts, but ill at ease in the Harding-Coolidge era, in which every departure from the petit-bourgeois norm in thinking was held up to condemnation or ridicule by the dominant organs of opinion. Apostles of material success like Ford and Edison were the heroes of the day. A schoolteacher named Scopes was prosecuted in Tennessee by that great political liberal William Jennings Bryan for expounding the theory of evolution, and the only public issue on which it was respectable to object to the current state of affairs was Prohibition. Satire, volubly expressed by Henry L. Mencken and his school, provided release for many. But those who were not satisfied with escape into bitter laughter were impressed by other protests, such as the British book which appeared early in the decade, *The Sickness of an Acquisitive Society* by R. H. Tawney (published in the United States under the title *An Acquisitive Society*). The financial extravaganza of the late years of the decade did indeed make it seem that our civilization had become obese and aged as well as anti-intellectual and without grace. The "New Era" appeared to be economically as well as morally and aesthetically due for an attack of coronary disease.

The attack came in 1929, and for three years the patient, though President Hoover frequently proclaimed that its recovery was "just around the corner," sank deeper and deeper into mortality. In 1932 it wavered between life and death. One quarter of the nation's labor force was unemployed; many people could not even get emergency relief; states and local

governments were bankrupt; the banking system was collaps-
ing. "Private enterprise," which had suffocated all values but
its own, now failed to serve even the values which its most
loyal adherents proclaimed. Instead of a "chicken in every
pot" and "two cars in every garage," there were empty pots
and garages—and little else to make men happy.

The émigrés had come back; they and the followers of intellectual and aesthetic pursuits who had stayed at home were
galvanized by this dramatic and sorry spectacle. Perhaps now
something might be done after all. It was only natural that
the most spectacular converts to communism should be among
the intellectuals, particularly those who through lack of experience were naïve about political and economic practices.
It offered them a logical creed which seemed to account for
everything. A doctrine and a program in which to believe satisfied their deep craving. But their motives were not those
which Marx attributed to a hungry proletariat; they were
moved in reality by the whole tradition of humanitarian and
aesthetic protest against the prevailing culture, which had
been expressed mainly by thinkers in deep disagreement with
Marx's materialist philosophy. In consequence they were unreliable converts; many, disgusted with the behavior of flesh-
and-blood Communist party members sooner or later drifted
away.

Much *was* done under the leadership of the democratic
aristocrat Franklin D. Roosevelt, who in his belief and practice
was as far as possible from the Marxist temper. Not only were
material injustices remedied and institutions changed, but for
a while it seemed that the nation would legally recognize the
importance of intellectually creative work. The WPA, among
its manifold activities, included a theater project, a writers'
project, an art project. This was too much for Congress, however; such "frills" were specially vulnerable to attack by those
who opposed the New Deal, and they were abolished long

before the WPA as a whole quietly passed away during World War II, when mass unemployment vanished.

Temporarily, war, postwar prosperity, and the threat of a final war of annihilation have supplied preoccupations so great as to submerge the centuries-old criticisms of the technological order as it was developed. Rightly so, for World War II was a defense of the democratic possibility to create something better, and World War III, if it comes, seems certain either to annihilate man altogether or at least to destroy all his technological advances and any modern culture whatsoever.

Yet the meta-materialistic creative spirit struggles on; if man and modern culture survive, that spirit will be heard from again. It will unceasingly search for answers to its questions: What is a good life for man? How can it be lived in modern civilization?

New Views of the Modern Malaise

The malaise of civilization has of course begun to be scientifically studied as well as poetically expressed. The sociologists, the psychiatrists, the anthropologists, and the philosophers are concerned with it. The questions which they pose to themselves largely concern the deep fissure in our civilization which has bothered the writers and artists. Tentative answers, indicated by various types of evidence, have been formulated. According to one theory, in cultures (as a rule primitive) where the adult experiences of the people are what their childhood training have led them to expect, where beliefs and practices are in accord, there seems to be little or no mental disease, at least of any of the types common among us. To be sure, the behavior of any normal member of such a tribe might seem neurotic or psychotic in civilized society, though this person is well adjusted to his own. To say this is not to say

that all well-integrated primitive cultures are, by the standards of Western culture, earthly paradises; some of them are
brutal, cruel, and stunted. But there are also primitive cultures which seem pleasant to the investigators, and in which
expectations and fulfillment are in accord.

The contrary is to some extent true in modern Western culture. Children, according to the code of beliefs to which lip-
service at least is usually given, are loved, protected, given a
feeling of security. Cooperation among them is encouraged.
Rivalry and competition exist, but they are not permitted to go
beyond decent bounds. The aim of all liberal education is to
expose children to the best in ideas, art, and morals. At the
end of the formative period boys and girls are plunged into a
culture in which these expectations are far from fulfilled. As
long as neither the expectations nor the culture are changed
there is bound to be painful adjustment. Even in childhood
malconditioned adults may introduce into the child's experience discordant elements which wreck his personality and his
inner security.

Another formulation of the rift between personality and society has been outlined by Erich Fromm. Speaking to an audience of Bennington College students about what W. H. Auden
has called the "age of anxiety," he distinguished three kinds
of anxiety. There is rational fear, caused by realistic dangers,
which is perfectly healthy and necessary. There is existential
or productive anxiety—the lot of weak and finite man looking
into the abyss of loneliness, which is also healthy, because "it
is one of the most important conditions for the unfolding of
our strength and productiveness." The aims common to all
the great religions, says Fromm, can be achieved only if men
allow themselves to feel this anxiety; it leads to success in
the art of living. The third kind, or irrational anxiety, which is
particularly characteristic of our age, he thinks, arises from
the repressing of more fundamental emotional needs in order
to "chase after success, power, comfort, and prestige, ready to

sacrifice everything else for the attainment of these goals."

It is the "marketing orientation," according to Fromm, which lies at the bottom of moral and human failure in the modern world. Man's self-esteem comes to depend on acceptance by others and a high price tag. "Commodity man hopefully displays his label," he emulates the smartest, newest model instead of being himself. If a man's highest value is success, "he may think he worships the God of love but actually he worships an idol."

"The consequence of this orientation is inevitable; it is a deep-seated anxiety, an anxiety which springs from the failure to develop our best and most specifically human powers, which in turn makes us afraid even of attempting to change our course or cease escaping from ourselves, and from our task." If anything like this is true, the goal of a commercial civilization turns out to be at odds with the goals advocated at all times by the great spiritual leaders of mankind. Mere getting on, mere change are not enough.

Humanity seems to be almost infinitely plastic in the long run, but not all individuals can adapt to rapid change in the course of a single lifetime. Since the strains of progress—or at least of change—give rise to the great discomforts in civilization, it is pertinent to ask what the change is leading to. No sensible person expects or wants a new Garden of Eden. Utopias have their uses in the world of the mind; but usually they turn out to be frauds when hopeful souls try to create them in practice. Nevertheless a charted course is necessary to give meaning both to difficulties and to triumphs. Must one accept the adventurous voyage of the human race simply as the meaningless wandering of a crew of amateur sailors? Since each of us will at some time perish in this ocean, must we do so with the thought that it makes no particular difference at what port the ultimate survivors arrive? Of all un-American attitudes, that would be the most traitorous to the national tradition.

6

THE ECONOMY OF TIME

A basic problem, both of economic theory and of economic practice, has long been to understand how scarce resources are allocated so as best to satisfy wants in the order of consumers' preference. Economical use of resources was the task of the self-sustaining or nearly self-sustaining family farm in American colonial and pioneer days. The family had land—including all the natural resources that were in it or on it, like wood, stone, minerals, water. It had the labor power of its members. It had tools, buildings, and other supplies, including perhaps some money savings, which represented the product of former labor applied to materials—in other words, capital. The thrifty and well-managed household was the one that made good use of these resources in order to supply its members with food, clothing, shelter, fuel, additions to its capital, or anything else the family might need. Good use meant attending first of all to the most important wants, and

then to the others in descending order, as long as the resources
held out.

The Economists' Account of Resource Allocation

Some resources, like air, economists call free goods; although essential, they are so abundant that they do not need
to be economized and so have no price. Land, in early America, was relatively abundant, but labor and capital were relatively scarce. Therefore more attention was devoted to increasing the efficiency with which labor was used, and to
building up and improving capital, than to getting the most
out of a given number of acres or preserving their fertility.

The commercial order grew up as transportation, communication, and increased specialization of production permitted
the development of purchase and sale—that is, of markets.
The market has been regarded by economic theorists as embodying an almost automatic method of resource allocation.
What consumers wanted most they would pay the most for,
provided it was scarce enough to command a high price. A
high price would give incentive to producers to make and sell
more of the most wanted articles. Thus the price mechanism
and the incentive of profit brought about the allocation of
resources in at least some rough correspondence with the pref-
erences of consumers, as long as the necessary resources were
abundant enough. Scarcer resources were, in effect, rationed
by the higher prices that could be charged for products made
from them.

An intricate logical pattern has been built up by economists
to account for the interplay of demand, supply, and prices in
a private-enterprise economy under laissez-faire, but the main
idea is clear enough without peering into the details.

Always, in their thinking, the economists of the classical
tradition have believed that land, labor, and capital were the
major classifications, including all resources that have a scar-

city value, as contrasted with free or non-economic goods. The formulation of economic thought, both on the part of theorists and on the part of businessmen, has been laid out on this three-dimensional framework.

In this respect classical economics is like classical physics, which structured its mental models in a three-dimensional universe of space. Modern physics, however, has found it necessary to add a fourth dimension—time. Of course the concept of time was frequently used by physicists before the four-dimensional universe was rounded out in theory, as in studies of speed, acceleration, force, and the like. But in his theory of relativity Einstein eventually showed that the time factor was always intimately associated with measurement; spatial dimensions might actually be altered when the time coordinate was considered.

Time as a Scarce Resource

The classical economic market analysis, in its elementary form, assumed for purposes of logic that the relationships among demand, supply, and price were to be considered as of a given moment—that is, the theory was static. This assumption was sometimes stated; often it was merely implied. But in applying the theory to the real world it was necessary to take into consideration what would happen over time. In other words, the static theory had to be supplemented by a dynamic one. An obvious need for this kind of reasoning arose in analyzing money markets, which involved the concept of the present value of capital that might be expected to increase over a period of years. Saving, too, was seen to involve the sacrifice of present satisfaction for the sake of future gain. Another, and more recent, application is the analysis of the businessman's expectation about such things as prices and profits, what it leads him to do, and how what he does will react on his own future (often contrary to his expectation).

Still, however, economic theorists have not absorbed the concept of time formally into their basic thinking, as physical theorists have done. Specifically, economists have not regarded time as a scarce resource, coordinate with land, labor, and capital, and have not developed their theory of resource allocation on this four-dimensional framework. Yet the technological revolution cannot be understood without reference to the time factor, which in practice has been involved from the very beginning. Still less could there be an economic theory appropriate to the present and future of a technological civilization without recognizing the immense and growing importance of time as a scarce resource.

As often, popular language anticipates scientific theory by its intuitive, common-sense phrases. The wage-earner does not refer to the employer as buying his labor; what the employer buys is his *time*. When the employee puts in extra work it is *overtime*, for which he is paid *time and a half*, or even *double time*. When the consumer appraises a commercial product he sometimes asks, "Is it worth the price," but more often, in appraising a project, "Is it worth *while?*"

When the employer or the engineer turns his attention to technical improvements, he thinks of them not just as devices by which more goods can be turned out or by which materials or capital can be economized, but as devices by which more can be done in a given time, or, to put the emphasis the other way, by which the same product can be produced in less time, and so time can be economized. The progress of labor welfare, in union terminology particularly, is measured not only by wages, but by "wages, *hours,* and conditions." Economists, engineers, and accountants, in measuring costs or advances in productivity, universally use the term *man-hours* or *man-days*.

Even corporate accounts, although they contain no specific references to time (except perhaps in mentioning the redemption dates of bond issues) make a distinction between "cur-

rent assets"—that is, those that can be realized in a short space
of time—and "fixed" or "other" assets, which could be turned
into cash, if at all, only over a longer period. "Depreciation" is
the loss of value of existing equipment reckoned on the basis
of its estimated years of useful life. The balance sheet itself is
supposed to represent the financial condition of the corpora-
tion as of a given day, and the fortunes of the business may
be measured by examining its successive balance sheets over
a period of years. The more recently introduced income statement, or profit-and-loss statement, reveals the details of the
revenue, the expenses, and the gain over a given period of
time—usually a year. Without the time factor, all such economic measurements would be impossible.

Economic statisticians are dependent on time series for
measurements and analysis of economic growth and cyclical
or other fluctuations. Price indexes, production indexes, indexes of employment, national income, and the rest all depend
on a view of the subject matter over a series of years or months.
Without such measurements involving a time factor, a large
part of the material of modern economic analysis could not
exist. To economize the time in which material gain can be
maximized is universally regarded as a test of economic welfare.

The Consumer of Time

More relevant, perhaps, to the points at issue in this book,
is the attitude of the individual toward the time at his disposal.
This, both popular speech and literary tradition give evidence,
long antedates modern improvements. "Time is money." We
"save" time, "spend" time, and "waste" time, just as we save,
spend, and waste money or material goods. When zest flags,
"time lies heavy on our hands," we "kill time."

What could be more melancholy than Shakespeare's

> Tomorrow, and tomorrow, and tomorrow
> Creeps in this petty pace from day to day
> To the last syllable of recorded time;
> And all our yesterdays have lighted fools
> The way to dusty death. . . .
> Life's but a walking shadow, a poor player,
> That struts and frets his hour upon the stage
> And then is heard no more.

Time, so viewed, is incomparably more precious than money or the material goods money can buy. To be a "poor player" in one's hour on the stage, to live briefly as "a walking shadow," is the ultimate tragedy.

To the individual, time is a scarce resource indeed. Each day fades to an end; Sunday follows Sunday; December, December. The clock ticks, the calendar counts from one to two, from two to three, from three to four, from four to five, like an old-fashioned class in elementary arithmetic, until each listener shall pass out of hearing and for him time shall cease. The cosmos may have no beginning and no end, but from that infinite deep no man can dip more than a tiny cupful.

Goods may pile up, traversable space can be extended. Even for one person there are no known limits to such expansion; time alone has a boundary guarded by relentless sentries.

The sense of passing time is probably not so keen among tribes which do not mark it with clocks or calendars. Animals seem to live an hour as if there were no past or future, to taste, smell, and feel it, to confront each pain or fear, each delight, with its full appropriate acceptance or rejection, and without remembrance for days that have passed or anticipation of days to come. No civilized being can match the lazy relaxation of the tiger or his furious activity. Man, however, who in the course of his social evolution has developed more of what is called intelligence, shows it by marking an event as it rises from its origins through a temporal sequence. He abstracts like events, he plays with cause and consequence in ways that lend time reality.

Measurements of time are essential to man's manipulations and creations. The seed must be planted at the right elevation of the sun and when soil conditions are right; it would never be planted at all if the cultivator did not expect that in a computable time it would bear fruit. What we do today we often do because we expect something to grow from it tomorrow. Work, which characterizes civilization, is activity directed to a future outcome that is expected to constitute a reward for the time spent in preparing for the result and awaiting it.

Time for Sale

Does the market system apportion time to the uses best fitted to satisfy human needs, as economists argued that it apportioned land, labor, and capital? In the era of the eleven- or twelve-hour working day and the singleminded pursuit of gain on the part of businessmen, most of a man's time was indeed devoted to earning a living or getting on and was indeed "spent" for material goods. The wage-earners sold their time so that they and their children could have something to eat, clothing to wear, and a place to live. These were essential. The busy profit-maker spent his time for the competitive success—or failure—which his abilities and his luck permitted.

Time—almost all they had outside the hours necessary for sleeping and eating—was allocated to producing and distributing the goods which consumers wanted or could be induced to buy. But the time itself was an irreplaceable resource. Many, looking back over a lifetime of drudgery, or of struggle for riches which they could not take with them, must have felt that in gaining a living they had lost a life.

Those few who piled up enough so that they or their children need no longer exchange time for material goods often did not know what to do with the time they thus had saved. They had learned few of the skills of getting their time's worth, outside the pursuits in which they had been engaged. The market system, emulsified in the prevailing culture, had spilled over almost the whole landscape. How could anything made, or done, but not salable, have value? Could not one buy anything or anybody one wanted—at a high enough price? And how could anyone maintain his self-respect without working? Working meant, of course, nothing but occupying oneself with producing or handling for sale.

These standards of value are revealed by the very epithet "idle" rich. If one was not busy making goods, or making money by manipulation of goods, he must be regarded as "idle," and to be "idle" was a sin against civilization. Poor idlers were immoral or unthrifty, hobos or wastrels; rich idlers were leeches on society. Even "unemployment" meant, and by traditional usage still means, being without employment at something for which one is paid in money or its equivalent. And even up to the early 1930s to be unemployed was regarded not so much a misfortune as a personal fault.

President Hoover and many of his supporters thought it treasonable to the code of rugged individualism to admit that the unemployed had a legal right to relief, or to pay such compensation out of the federal treasury. The plight of the jobless should, they thought, be relieved by charity, private and local; but to embody in legislation the principle that unemployment was socially caused and should be socially compensated violated the stern command supposedly enunciated to the Virginia settlers by Captain John Smith: "He that will not work, neither shall he eat."

Labor-Saving Is Time-Saving

Treacherous as a fifth column, technological advance was all the while sapping the fortifications of this early system of

market values. Labor-saving devices, proudly welcomed by
the leaders and supporters of the business system, were in
essence time-saving devices. At first the saved time was almost wholly channeled not to shorter hours for those who in-
dividually did the work, but to larger quantity of product.
Time and goods, like energy and matter, are ultimately interchangeable. The enlarged product was at first devoted partly
to sustaining a rapid growth in population, partly to an expansion of capital equipment so that still more goods could be
made in the future. But in the end, through the very mechanism of the market itself, the wage-earners enforced their
preference for a different division of the gain. They wanted
less "work" and more time of their own, time not for sale. Perhaps few of them understood that shorter hours meant fewer
goods and services than otherwise they might have had. But in
any case goods and services were being multiplied so rapidly
that they could have more things and more time besides. They
determinedly chose, and collectively bargained for, more time
away from the job. Those who could not enforce this bargain
in the labor market eventually obtained it by democratic political action which established legal maximum hours of work.

Time Bought by the Workers

One of the arguments advanced by labor spokesmen for the
shorter work day was that it would, by forcing the employment of more persons to do a given amount of work, decrease
the ranks of the unemployed. Economists have questioned
whether this result could be expected. Certainly, in a society
where technological improvement was not occurring, shorter
working hours without corresponding reduction in pay would
mean higher costs per unit of product, which in turn would
mean higher prices to consumers, which in turn might limit
markets and so decrease employers' demand for labor. Entirely aside from the economic validity of the labor argument,

however, this illuminates a general shift in values which the
workers' voice emphasized. There was nothing intrinsically
moral or desirable about "working," as they experienced work.
On the contrary, everybody would gain by working as little
time as possible. Unemployment was evil not because it
denied its victims the privilege of working, but because it
denied them the privilege of earning. To transmute unemployment into shorter working time for the employed would be to
transmute lead into gold.

This sense of the value of time, of the possibility of balanc-
ing time against material reward in making choices, has penetrated far up the hierarchy of business. To be sure, as one
goes up the ladder many compensations aside from purely material ones are offered for successful work. Prestige, social position, the fascination of power, in many cases the interest of
the work itself, are enhanced in the higher echelons. Offset-
ting disadvantages are worry, the load of responsibility, the
peril of mistakes. But large material rewards indeed must now
be offered to keep top executives on the job. Partly this is a
result of the scarcity of competent candidates. Probably to an
even greater degree, however, it is because the executive, like
the wage-earner, begins to question whether a larger quantity
of worldly goods might not be bought at too high a price—a
price in time which might better have been spent otherwise.

Men at or near the top of their vocations are frequently
allowed a good deal of leeway in devoting time to matters
which have only a remote connection with the jobs for which
they are hired. They are given leaves of absence to accept
governmental or other public responsibilities, engage in philanthropic, artistic, or other activities galore, and work for
associations, educational organizations, and the like which
may indeed produce something of great social value but make
no profit and do not recompense with money those who manage them. In the markets of today the demand for paid labor
has to compete vigorously with the worker's demand to allo-

cate his own time, from the bottom to the top of the labor army. If this were not so, Western civilization would be impoverished indeed.

Unsold Time Is Productive

If the United States had to depend for its welfare solely on private enterprise in producing goods and services which can be sold to consumers at a profit, some of the deepest and most pressing wants of its citizens would go unsatisfied. Many of these wants are met by non-profit governmental activities—such as a large part of education, scientific research, public-health work, highways, protection against disturbances of the peace and foreign enemies, social security, and the like. Government employees now number about 13 out of every 100 in the labor force. Their proportion has been steadily growing and is likely to grow more. But this is an old story. What is usually overlooked is the immense contribution made to the civilization by private institutions of a non-profit character and still more by private individuals spending at least part of their time at something that is not sold for a profit.

The enterprise of individuals has no more important function in modern American civilization than the allocation of unsold time to satisfy wants the demand for which is not registered in any market by the clink of money in the cash register. The compilers of statistics have not counted the detailed allocation of this immense resource, but it is as essential a basis of the economy as crops, iron and steel, plants and machinery, and workers on their jobs.

The Order of Scarcity

Only scarce resources, according to theory, have an economic value. Those not scarce may be had for the asking—or even without asking. Scarcity and abundance are of course

relative terms. A good can be either scarce or abundant only
in relation to the demand for it. And any scarce commodity
may be more scarce or less scarce than another.

If time be added to land, labor, and capital as a basic category of scarce resources, how do the four rank in relative
scarcity in the United States?

At the beginning of the white settlement in North America,
land, including all natural resources, was relatively abundant;
labor and capital relatively scarce. In consequence land was
cheap or indeed sometimes costless, labor and capital relatively expensive. This relationship continued well through the
nineteenth century. One could earn more as a worker or an
investor than in the old world, but the landlord was so much
at a disadvantage that all the attempts to set up a feudal system based on landed estates eventually failed. Whatever
agrarian revolution was necessary in the new country occurred
so long ago that it scarcely left a trace in the nation's history or
tradition. (This fact alone marks a subtle but deep difference
between North American culture and that of most of Europe
and Asia.) It is true that much money was made by specu-
lators in land as population increased and the price of acreage
rose in both country and city, but this is a different matter.

As for time, it certainly was no less scarce in the new country than either labor or capital. Americans wanted results in
a hurry; there was so much to do that quicker ways of doing
them were always at a premium. Other peoples have habit-
ually thought of Americans as hustlers; Americans have
thought of other peoples as slow and somnolent. Whenever
the new civilization was reproached for lack of refinement or
tradition, the customary reply was, We are young, we are too
busy; give us time.

Since the last accession of new territory, the absolute number of square miles has not increased, and the natural deposits certainly have been diminished, while the population
has been multiplying. In this literal sense land and resources

have become more scarce than either labor or capital, and
the prices or rents of favorably situated tracts or of limited
resources have correspondingly risen. Technology, however,
has intervened to moderate the costs to consumers. So greatly
has the output of crops per acre increased that, barring the
intervention of droughts or governmental controls, there is
still a relative abundance and in some cases even an unsalable
surplus of food and fibers. Technology, too, has continually
found new ways of increasing the efficiency of scarce natural
resources or has devised substitutes for them. Aside from the
cases where restrictive monopoly of narrowly limited resources can operate, people are not pinched by scarcities.

Labor, in the sense of the number of people willing to work
for pay, grew rapidly in supply with the extraordinary increase of population, but never, for long, faster than the demand for the product. In more recent decades population
growth has shown a tendency to slow down. But here technology has been at work too. If one measures the value of
labor by hourly wages received, one would have to conclude
that in the United States labor is still scarcer than anywhere
else in the world. But the real cost to the employer is not
that of an hour's work, but what he must pay for the contribution of labor to a unit of output. If technical improvement
doubles output per man-hour, the cost of that man-hour to
the employer is halved per unit of output, provided hourly
wages remain the same. In this sense labor has become abundant; in most highly mechanized industries the United States
can meet the competition, in a world market, of other nations
in which the wages per hour are much lower. What is perhaps
even more to the point, the demand of the domestic market
for goods as a whole almost never exceeds the output of industry and agriculture except in war or extreme inflation.
Unemployment is fully as frequent as a general labor shortage.

The nation's stock of capital has increased of course more

rapidly than its land, and even more rapidly than the labor supply. For many years this was a consequence of the type of mechanization which substituted capital for labor in the productive process. In more recent years the volume of capital has not increased so rapidly as before, but the efficiency of the equipment has been so improved that, as in the case of labor, a unit of capital can contribute much more to output than a unit of previous years. Capital in consequence has in the real sense become as abundant as labor, if not more so. A tendency toward slowly shrinking return per dollar of invested capital gives evidence of this abundance.

Time Is the Scarcest Resource

The efficiency of time has been much multiplied with the improvement of the whole productive process. As a consequence the population has been able to receive both more goods and more time away from work. But the demands on this free time have more than correspondingly increased. Who has enough time to do all that he thinks is required of him, or all that he would like to do insofar as the choice is entirely his own? A multiplicity of possible occupations compete for the time available to anyone; few Americans are weighed down by time hanging heavy on their hands.

In an economic as well as in a philosophical or poetic sense, time must now be regarded as the scarcest of all the categories of basic resources. This difference is likely to become exaggerated if the future stages of the technological revolution fulfill the present promise. Already goods regarded as the main necessities have become so abundant that it is difficult to increase their sales faster than the population grows. This is certainly true of food staples and of all the clothing necessary for warmth and comfort. Of shelter it is not yet true, but even this want may be satiated in the course of a few more genera-

tions. The principal growing markets are for goods and services used by people in their time off the job—these highly
diverse wants may expand and change for many decades to
come.

If time were unlimited, there could be no end to the potential demand for goods. But suppose the extreme case—suppose that nobody had to spend any hours at all in production
of products for sale; suppose "work" were all done by automatic machines. Still there would be a limit, within any year,
of the amount of time a given population would have in which
to use what might be sold to them. Add up all the automobiles,
television sets, fishing rods and lures, golf clubs, tennis rackets,
boats, garden tools, cameras, cellar workshop equipment,
books and magazines, musical instruments—make the list as
long as you like—that a whole population could possibly use
in all the waking time available in a year, and you would get
a tremendous but still finite amount.

As that limit is approached, it will appear even more clearly
than now that technological civilization, if it continues to
endure and to increase output per man-hour at a compound-
interest rate, is gradually making goods more abundant than
the time in which to consume or enjoy them. What has been
called the "non-productive" time of the worker has been much
increased and may increase still more, but there are no more
than 24 hours a day and 365 days a year.

Technology has mastered the art of saving time, but not the
art of spending it. The situation which man under technology
is approaching emphasizes the problem of economizing not so
much land, labor, and capital as the time which is not devoted
to earning a living. This is the ultimate gain that man may
receive from the technological revolution. Will he allocate
it in such a way as to satisfy his needs in the order of their importance? Are there not wants that a market system cannot
exploit? How will man proceed to allocate his time in satisfy-

ing them without the aid of prices and markets? Is it not clear that any effort to do so must emphasize a different set of values than those dominant in the nineteenth and early twentieth centuries? Will the consequences not be a change in civilization so great that it will mark the beginning of a new instar?

7

THE PURSUIT OF HAPPINESS

Those who have felt the discontents of Western civilization have been disappointed in many attempts either to remold it quickly or to escape from it. Like raftsmen adrift on a flooded river, they cannot quell the racing water itself; the best they can seem to do is either to make for an eddy which offers momentary protection but sets them apart from the main stream, or perilously to shoot the rapids in the hope that they may with skill and good luck preserve life on any terms at all.

Utopian Disappointments

The early utopians expected that by putting their ideas into practice in small groups they could induce imitation and regenerate society. This was a reasonable inference from the set of ideas on which their thinking was based—the "enlight-

enment" of the eighteenth-century philosophers. It was a
logical, if somewhat naïve, doctrine. The physical scientists
had discovered laws of nature which permitted many inventions and seemed to open a boundless prospect for mastery
by man over the physical universe. If, in spite of this magnifi-
cent breakthrough into virgin territories of knowledge and
power, men were still miserable and wicked, the reason must
be that they had not discovered the "natural laws" of human
behavior. To discover these laws the philosophers consulted
what they imagined to have been the primitive state of man
—that is, the state of nature before, as they thought, man was
corrupted by mistaken controls and ideas. In the primitive
state, they supposed, man was reasonable, cooperative, and
good. Give reason and goodness a chance, and in their own
generation human behavior would become so much more in
accord with natural law than was the grasping selfishness of
the world they knew that reason and goodness could easily
prevail.

Of course re-education was necessary, and a different structure of social and economic relations. But these requirements
surely could be provided in a community of dedicated souls,
small but with enough in number to provide their own necessities. Robert Owen, the British textile manufacturer, tried
it in New Harmony, Indiana. The Transcendentalists tried
it at Brook Farm in Massachusetts. These are only the best
known of a number of such attempts, made in America with
sundry volunteers and a variety of organizational principles
and beliefs. Some of these ventures quickly disintegrated,
others lasted longer, but none stimulated much imitation.
Apparently the general population was not eager to sacrifice
the temptations or the standards of the world as it was for the
chance to live solely by reasonableness, cooperation, and
nobility of spirit.

A few religious orders seeking salvation did better, but
only under the discipline of what they supposed was a di-

vinely ordained way of life and under the regulation of some
theocratic organization. Outside of those religious institutions
which had survived from medieval culture, the most notable
of these groups in the United States was the Mormons. Their
pilgrimage did carry them to a region so remote that they
won freedom from persecution and a chance to build their
own society. But before long the main stream of American
civilization flowed about them again, and they became
adapted to it, rather than exerting much influence of their
own on the national culture.

Groups with beliefs dissenting from those generally accepted have, here and there, established freedom to differ,
but they survive, as a rule, by excluding from their ranks
what they disapprove rather than by eliminating evil from
their environment. Their converts are relatively few, their
contributions to social change small.

Individual Escape

Individuals like Thoreau, Henry James, the émigrés of the
1920s, and others sought escape to preserve their personal
independence—and not without thought of the values they
hoped to perpetuate or enhance for the society they temporarily left. Escapes on a smaller and less publicized scale
are frequent among intellectuals, artists, craftsmen. Fortu-
nately, in our diverse and confused society, there are many
crannies into which the ingenious may crawl to be undis-
turbed while they conduct life and thought more or less in
their own way. Without some exiles to whom at need the
main body of citizens can listen, or whom it can invite to
return, any civilization is the poorer. To seek personal salvation alone may be on occasion the best way to serve society. But escape is not a high road to social change. The
voice crying in the wilderness may carry far over the centuries, but its immediate hearers are few.

The apparent futility of those who have tried to reconstitute the going institutions by persuasion or reform from within is one of the main bulwarks of Marxist doctrine. Nothing much can be changed, according to this body of ideas, before a revolutionary overturn in society as a whole, on the basis of which a new beginning can be made and a new direction taken. And when this overturn occurs, all the hampering ideological structure of the old civilization must be rigidly excluded. An entire people must be vigorously re-educated to the new order. This argument has appealed strongly since the 1920s to many disillusioned reformers.

Enforced Regeneration

What can follow from accepting the Marxist revolutionary formula may be observed at work in states where the Soviet system has gained ascendancy. The basis of all else is a strictly disciplined and exclusive governing apparatus, composed of those who will be loyal to officially approved doctrine. The most important task of this party is at all costs to gain and to keep unlimited power. Thus the essence of the "revolution" is the imposition by dictatorial methods of what is expected to be a way of living and thinking. The result, of course, is no social revolution at all, in any real sense. In method, if not entirely in measures, it is a return to the enslavement of man and of man's mind, against which humanistic revolutionaries have struggled for centuries. To impose regeneration and freedom is a contradiction in terms.

Is it necessary, however, to undergo a temporary restriction of freedom in order to arrive at the material basis of a fine and free civilization? Communists, both before and after Marx, have aspired to a society so productive that there would be plenty for all; only in such a society could the egalitarian distributive aim first announced by the utopians be realized— "to each according to his needs, from each according to his ability." Marx devoted a large part of his analytic talents to an attempt to prove the proposition that capitalism could not possibly produce abundance for all in spite of its technical proficiency. This is the basic economic theory by which the expropriation of private owners of productive property has been defended.

Many opponents of socialism have contented themselves with the reply that socialized industry either could not produce at all, or could not produce efficiently because of the absence of financial incentives for investment of capital and the absence of competitive selection of the more efficient producers.

Both the Marxist and the conventional anti-Marxist positions have now been proved fallacious by the record. In the United States at least, markets have not shrunk but have grown tremendously because a major share of the product has been distributed to the industrial workers and others not participating directly in industrial profits. American businessmen have found the domestic market so profitable that it is even difficult to convince many of them that they have much to gain by selling abroad. And in Russia—and in other nations as well—socialized industries have managed not only to produce but to increase production rapidly. The gains of the Soviet Union in industrialization have been so great that fear is expressed by some who are concerned with military potential that in the course of time Russia and her satellites may possess an industrial base for warfare outranking even that of the United States.

Socialism Invests More Than Capitalism

Ironically enough, the debaters have in one important respect exchanged positions. Though statistics of Russian production and income are much more scanty and less reliable than those of the United States, virtually all competent stu-

dents agree that the citizen of the "socialized" economy not
only suffers from shocking lack of goods, if his level of living
be judged by American standards—as might be expected in
a nation which adopted the industrial revolution long after
it became established here—but that his gain in real income
during the past twenty or thirty years has been at a far
slower pace than that of American workers. And the main
reason, strange to say, is that the "socialized" economy de-
votes a much larger part of its growing productive power to
new capital investment than does the "capitalist" economy.
It is the Soviet state that deprives its workers of present enjoyment in the interest of rapid accumulation, the American
economy that shares the fruits of production abundantly with
its workers as it goes along. Indeed, one of the chief charges
now leveled at the Soviet economy is that it saves and invests
too much; in the interest of growth it imposes too great a
sacrifice on the present generation.

As far back as anything like reliable figures go—that is, to
about 1870—the United States has never in any decade invested more than about 7 per cent of its net national product
in new productive facilities, and the rate has shown a downward tendency. The remaining 93 per cent—except for the
investment necessary to renew existing plant—has consisted
of goods and services for consumers. Official Soviet figures of
the increase in production since before World War I are suspected of having an upward bias, but at least they do show
something of the relationship between the product of heavy
industry and that of light industry making consumers' goods.
In 1913, before the revolution, about one-third of the total
output consisted of productive facilities and two-thirds consisted of consumers' goods. In 1940, the products of heavy
industry were reported to be almost sixteen times greater than
in 1913, while consumer-goods output had grown somewhat
less than five times. Now two-thirds of the gross output comes
from heavy industry. During World War II consumer goods

suffered a further setback; after it they regained some lost
ground.

The citizens of a free economy apparently have not been
willing to allocate to savings and investment anywhere near
so large a percentage of what they produce. Their preference
has been registered not in votes but in the way they divide
their incomes, in a free retail market, between consumption
and savings. Only where the distribution of the fruits of production is controlled by a central authority can the gains be
channeled so largely to new capital as in Russia.

America Closest to Material Abundance

The citizens of the American economy are now far closer
to material abundance than the citizens of the Soviet Union.
Though they are not building up their capital at so urgent a
rate, they are increasing their productivity rapidly. With their
long head start, the chances are that they will arrive approximately at the Communist ideal of abundance for all without
ever having adopted the Communist creed, and will do so
long before the adherents of communism get there. Wars,
little or big, may of course retard or destroy the advance of
both, but can give no advantage in the race to either side.

The American economy, we have seen, may within the next
eighty years arrive at an average family income of $25,000
(in 1953 dollars), if it repeats the rate of income growth of
the past eighty years. It can do this, presumably, without
depriving consumers year by year of more than about 7 per
cent of the net national income in order to enlarge the productive establishment.

The Russians, though their rate of investment, and hence
of advance in productive capacity, is now more rapid than
ours, start from a much lower base. Paul A. Baran, using what
figures exist, estimated that in 1940 the total outlay in Russia
on consumer goods, divided by the population of about 198

million, showed a per capita consumption equivalent to about
$153 a year. A similar calculation for the United States in the
same year indicates per capita consumption of about $600.
Such estimates are exceedingly sketchy, especially for Russia,
but other observations would indicate that the average Russian consumer hardly could buy more than one-fourth of the
amount of goods available to the average American consumer.

As sailors say, a stern chase is a long chase. If the authorities who control production and distribution in the Soviet
Union allow the consuming public to share more than before
in the gains of production, that much less will be available for
investment and hence for long-term growth. No nation, however strong its dictatorship, could without great risk keep its
people from sharing sooner or later more fully in its output
than Soviet consumers have shared in recent years. Yet to
allow them to consume as large a percentage of what they
make as do American citizens would imply that as long as we
maintain our present rate of growth they could never catch
us. For their yearly additions to productive capacity would
in that case be no greater a percentage of their smaller national product than our additions to capacity would be of our
larger product.

Let us suppose, to take an example, that since 1940 the
Soviet citizen's disposable income had been allowed to increase about 2 per cent a year—or as much as the American
citizen's disposable income—and that this rate will continue
indefinitely in both cases. Obviously the increase is com-
pounded. The Soviet citizen started with a per capita spending power of, say, $150, the American with $600. If you deposit $150 at 2 per cent compound interest it can never
become equal to $600 deposited on the same day at the same
rate of interest. Indeed, the difference between the two sums
will become wider instead of narrower as the years pass.

The Way Out Is Through

In any case, Americans have no reason to abandon their own line of development for another, if what concerns them most is to gain material abundance at the earliest possible moment. In this respect at least they have the immense good fortune of occupying the farthest outpost in the technological advance of Western civilization. They should, however, take care that their economic growth continues with at least reasonable regularity. They cannot afford the halting disorganization of another great depression like that of the 1930s. They cannot allow basic scientific research to shrivel up either through lack of funds and education or through security measures which interrupt necessary communication among scientists both within the nation and internationally. They must beware of anti-intellectual influences, of unnecessary barriers to change and flexibility. In particular, they must improve the quality of their education, while at the same time they prepare to educate more fully a much larger part of the population. Growth in productivity such as the American nation has enjoyed does not occur automatically; it is the result of widely shared competence, knowledge, and energy.

Certainly those who value mainly the non-material qualities of civilization can have no better hope for posterity than to see the technological revolution through, while in their own times they do what they can. The changes which seem to be imminent should offer increasing scope for the kind of values they favor.

If one is concerned about the effects of repetitive routine on the personality of the worker, he may take heart from the fact that the tedium and monotony are rapidly being taken over by machines, which do not mind them. More and more, the jobs left are those which involve direction of whole processes, invention, understanding, application of highly developed skills. More and more, the demand is for trained professionals in non-industrial pursuits.

If one is concerned about the competitive self-seeking of a business society, he may take some comfort from the fact that the competition for the bare essentials of a living and for favor of the powerful seems to be much more savage in the Soviet Union than in the United States, although in Russia business competition in the American sense is outlawed. The rough edges of economic rivalry wear smoother as want becomes less intense, and doorways for advance without stepping on the toes of others are opened wider.

A Possible "Stationary State"

More important in the long run, however, is that in the United States people are limiting their participation in the commercial-industrial system, at least for an increasing part of their time. They prefer to take a large share of the higher standards of living which technological advance permits in the form of less time on the paid job, and hence of more time to do whatever they like. This tendency is not likely to stop short at a forty-hour week or a thirty-five-hour week. There may never come a point at which everybody will say, Now I have all the goods and services I want, or at least all those capable of being bought with the proceeds of selling the time I wish to devote to that purpose. But that goal, experience has shown, is more and more narrowly being approximated by more and more people. At least they have found what they regard as better uses than earning a living for a large part of their time. Eventually they may arrive at a point where their effective demand for commercial goods will grow so slowly that economic progress in the traditional sense of enlarged output and population will virtually cease.

This possible outcome has been regarded with foreboding

by many economists, from Ricardo to the modern proponents of the idea that the American economy is in danger of stagnation—an idea prevalent in the 1930s. But at least one great economic thinker, John Stuart Mill, looked on the "stationary state" as a goal to be desired. In Book IV of his *Principles of Political Economy*, Mill declared:

> It is scarcely necessary to remark that a stationary condition of capital and population implies no stationary state of human improvement. There would be as much scope as ever for all kinds of mental culture, and more and more social progress; as much for improving the Art of Living, and much more likelihood of its being improved, when minds ceased to be engrossed by the art of getting on. Even the industrial arts might be as earnestly and as successfully cultivated, with the sole difference, that instead of serving no purpose but the increase of wealth, industrial improvements would produce their legitimate effect, that of abridging labor.

Mill, unlike Marx, foresaw no catastrophic crisis or necessary doom for capitalism, but he did foreshadow reforms and changes, many of which have in fact occurred. At least for Western and democratic industrial civilization, he was a far more discerning prophet than Marx. His idea of a future state in which the art of getting on may retreat before the art of living is much closer to realization now than a century ago. Who shall say that, in the course of the uninterrupted evolution of technology in a free society, it may not yet be realized? Is not this the very outcome our civilization has been seeking—in many ways devious and unconscious, in many ways more direct? And is it not, in view of the record and tendencies now evident, at least materially possible?

What Is the Art of Living?

It remains, of course, to specify in what the art of living may consist, and whether people are likely to practice it.

Once the curse of Adam is moderated—that he must earn his bread by the sweat of his brow—what other discipline can mold and direct him? The challenge of a future in which all may have the necessities of life without sacrificing for them more than a bare minimum of time is indeed startling. But it seems to be upon us.

And is not this after all what from the beginning has been implied in the American myth of natural rights? We have, imperfectly but with conviction, preserved and extended the right to life, and even that more subtle and ill-defined birthright, the right to liberty. If we manage to keep these in the future, we shall certainly have to devote more scrutiny than in the past to that third most perplexing and most elusive of the human rights enumerated in the Declaration of Independence—the right to the pursuit of happiness.

The right is of course to pursue, not to achieve. Many have learned that although material necessities may be essential for happiness, they are not enough. Certainly happiness easily eludes those who singlemindedly pursue wealth or power. In what does it consist, and how may it be experienced? Perhaps not at all on this earth, or perhaps only fleetingly. But it is literally true that millions of persons are, for the first time in human history, being freed from imposed miseries and obligations so that they may try to find out for themselves how to live well and fully. This is indeed a revolution. Conceivably it can lead to disaster. Man may not be capable of disciplining himself within so large an area of freedom. Insofar as he succeeds, however, he must produce a civilization the like of which has never been seen, and which dreamers have scarcely been able to imagine. The prospect embodies a challenge capable of engaging the utmost dedication of all who care about their own future or that of their children, their nation, and, ultimately, their world.

8

DO WE NEED
A LEISURE CLASS?

Thorstein Veblen, in his *Theory of the Leisure Class* (1899), ridiculed the behavior of those in American civilization who either had or aspired to the economic means to afford something beyond the main essentials of life. They were, he argued, concerned mainly with "pecuniary emulation" or the "desire of everyone to excel everyone else in the accumulation of goods." Not so much the need and use of goods themselves was the consideration, but the distinction which comes with possessing more than others. If, as he declared, such behavior set the goals for people in general, "however widely, or equally, or 'fairly' it may be distributed, no general increase of the community's wealth can make any approach to satiating this need."

Along with pecuniary emulation, one of the chief marks of distinction was, Veblen wrote, "conspicuous leisure"; not leisure for its own sake, but leisure which could be contrasted

with the hard work of others, leisure occupied in such showy
ways that it set off those who had it from the common herd.
Likewise the goods and services purchased had a value over
and above their plain utility; what was aimed at was "conspicuous consumption."

These values he illustrated from the dress of well-to-do
families, the occupations of their women members, the
amusements of the rich. The high silk hat, the stiffly starched
linen, the bonnets, corsets, silks and satins, the insubstantial
footwear—all such items were valued surely not for any aesthetic satisfaction but because they advertised the fact that
the wearers could not possibly be expected to perform any
manual, dirty, or menial tasks or to go anywhere on their own
feet. They were, in a sense, the distinctive uniform of the
leisure class. The lavish entertainments, the palatial houses
and estates, the retinues of servants, were surely dedicated
not to the ease and pleasure of the owners so much as to dis-
play of their eminence in the social scale. No man's wife
could be suspected of doing the housework without marking
him as of humble station.

This whole set of customs, which, it seemed to Veblen, set
the values of American life from top to bottom, he compared
with the institutions of barbaric cultures. The honorific
classes in such cultures had always been those who performed no utilitarian services. They were warriors, priests,
rulers, set off by their garb and pursuits from the common
folk who did the work. Indeed, *not to do anything useful* was
essential to a high station in society in America as in earlier
barbaric states.

The leisure class nevertheless had its function—to provide
a motive for the struggle for wealth and the competitive pursuits of the going system. Without it, capital accumulation
and endless increase of markets might have languished. But
by implication Veblen raised the question whether a society
devoted to getting on and keeping up exhibited intrinsic

worth, whether such "progress" indeed had any democratic or
other justification.

Veblen's view of the leisure class was strongly influenced
by puritanical assumptions. It implied by contrast that production of essentials ought to be the basis of society, and that
anything outside of this was vanity. Similar standards he
later applied in his *Theory of Business Enterprise*, in which
he argued that business and financial leaders made their
gains not by facilitating but by restricting production, and
in his *Engineers and the Price System*, which held out hope
that engineers and workers together might reform society
because both, unlike businessmen, were interested in enlarging the production of useful goods and so fulfilling the promise of a technological age.

Leisure Classes Have Their Uses

Whatever may have been the case with the American leisure class of the 1890s, thinkers have not usually been so
skeptical as Veblen of contributions that may be made to
civilization by an elite which does not have to spend its days
in unremitting manual labor. The cultural heritage of the
Western world would be poor indeed without the intellectual
and aesthetic achievements made possible partly because
creative workers had the time to devote to their callings, and
partly because a class, usually of aristocratic origin, had the
means to support, and the cultivated leisure to appreciate,
great works. This is not to say that creators were usually rich
men or that wisdom never sprang from the common people.
But it would be hard to name a period rich in contributions
to philosophy, science, literature, or the arts which was not
also a period in which at least a part of the population had
means and leisure above that necessary for a bare living.

The philosophers, poets, mathematicians, architects, and
sculptors of ancient Greece flourished at such a time, and

without them modern civilization would certainly be impoverished, if indeed it could have arisen at all. In ancient Greece the manual work was done by slaves, most of them war captives or the descendants of captives, and by free artisans who had no voting rights. The citizens were largely owners of landed estates and, at a later period, successful merchants. It was their democracy which formed the leading public for, and directly paid the expenses of, the creative minds and their works. Surely even such an iconoclast as Veblen himself could scarcely argue that members of the Athenian leisure class were concerned with nothing but outshining one another in pecuniary emulation, conspicuous consumption, and conspicuous waste.

The Aristocratic Tradition

On the contrary, the landed aristocracy resented and opposed the gain-seeking of the merchants and moneylenders, their apparent undermining of hallowed tradition, civic harmony, moderation, and justice. Plato was perhaps the most eminent spokesman of the aristocracy; he himself did not have to work for his living but sustained himself modestly from an inheritance. He argued, as every reader of the *Republic* knows, for a state ruled by officials selected from wellborn candidates by competitive examination, specially educated for their duties, and supported from the general store of wealth. A city-state, he thought, should not be allowed to grow too large, for then the inhabitants would be tempted to seek too many luxuries and strive for unlimited accumulation of wealth—the very traits that Veblen later satirized.

Plato proposed that wealth be held in common. But this proposal was in essence a defense of aristocratic virtues against the corruptions of a mercantile society, not socialism in the modern sense of elevating a proletariat. For Plato agreed with the general judgment that not only slaves but

free artisans were unfit for citizenship since their occupations engrossed their minds and often deformed their bodies.
To carry on government and the other arts of life was a full-
time job, not possible for those engaged in industry. In other
words, a leisure class (though not one absorbed in getting
on) was Plato's main reliance for a good society. There was
indeed such a class in Athens, though Athens suffered from
discord and corruption which Plato, with his aristocratic leanings, disapproved. He, like Veblen centuries later, disliked
the ignobility of an acquisitive society. Veblen differed with
Plato mainly about the desirability of participation in democracy by the workers.

Aristotle, though more scientific than Plato in his habit of
drawing conclusions from observation rather than from some
inner light substantiated by logic, agreed with him in opposing the accumulation of wealth by profit-seeking commerce
and the charging of interest on loans, and in excluding from
the rights of citizenship the actual workers in agriculture,
industry, and trade, largely on the ground that they lacked
the necessary leisure. He disagreed with Plato's judgment
that property should be held in common, but thought that it
should be devoted to the general use, "and the special business of the legislator is to create in men this benevolent dis-
position."

The aristocratic tradition in ancient Rome, too, favored a
skilled and responsible governing class—a class the achievements of which in law and statecraft have contributed greatly
to modern wisdom. At the same time the Roman philosophers
warned against self-indulgence and luxury on the part of the
patricians and wealthy merchants. And, like spokesmen for
other ancient ruling classes, the Roman thinkers found little
dignity in manual labor, trade, or money-lending. Cicero
declared in *de Officiis* that it was unbecoming to a gentleman
to engage in "the means of livelihood of all hired workmen
whom we pay for mere manual labor, not for artistic skill;

for in their case the very wages they receive is a pledge of their slavery." Here is something beyond a mere prejudice against working with the hands, work that might indeed be gentlemanly in artistic pursuits; here is something that comes closer to the heart of the matter—disapproval of labor which is not self-directed but rather is drudgery performed for pay.

"Vulgar," wrote Cicero, "we must consider those also who buy from wholesale merchants to retail immediately; for they would get no profits without a great deal of downright lying; and verily there is no action that is meaner than misrepresentation. . . . But the professions in which either a high degree of intelligence is required or from which no small benefit to society is derived—medicine and architecture, for example, and teaching—these are proper for those whose social position they become." Importers or exporters Cicero accepted if they gained fortunes without misrepresentation and, becoming satisfied to make no more, bought country estates. "Of all the occupations by which gain is secured, none is better than agriculture, none more profitable, none more delightful, none more becoming to a freeman."

Such sentiments fairly represent the aristocratic tradition, from that day to this. Typical of the ruling leisure class in almost all ages is the proprietor of an estate, who enjoys a sufficient income derived from the provision of common necessities, yet who has time to devote to public affairs, governmental or cultural.

In medieval times the courts of the landed nobility were often centers of culture and tradition. The Church itself acquired great landed estates and became a patron of arts and letters; it was as well a refuge of knowledge and of ethics in troubled times. Its hierarchy included not only the poor and lowly friars but dignitaries and princes, who were in effect members of the leisure class in the sense that they did not need to use their time making a living and hence were free to devote themselves to matters of greater significance.

During the Renaissance the princes of the Italian city-states and their retainers devoted much of the wealth, which had come to their communities through trading, to encourage an almost unprecedented flowering of creativeness. Here the rebirth of science, art, and philosophy laid the basis for modern advances and cast a wide influence throughout Europe.

Contributions to American Standards

In France the encyclopedists, before the revolution overthrew the monarchy and the nobility, depended largely on men of wealth and station for support of the ideas of democracy, liberty, and scientific humanism which became the immediate heritage of the American Republic. Together with other European scholars, and particularly British thinkers, they fired the minds of the leaders of the American revolution. And in the United States, Washington, Jefferson, Madison, and Monroe, themselves landed proprietors, were leaders in governing the new nation, formulating its policies and expressing its aspirations. From the North, professional men and cultivated members of merchant families such as John Adams were national leaders.

Until the time of Andrew Jackson the governing echelons of the new nation were largely recruited from the ranks of gentlemen, who, though they were in their thinking the radicals of their day, carried on the work of democracy with due regard for aristocratic virtues. It may be that part of the reason for any subsequent vulgarity of American values, felt by American and foreign critics alike, was that in this country there was not, and could not be, a stable leisure class in the traditional sense of one which came by its wealth and traditions without having to make them anew every generation—typically a landed gentry. Only such a class, secure in its privilege, did not have to worry about getting on or dealing with competitors. Its members were in a position, if they had the capacity and the will, to devote themselves to the art of life and set the tone of a civilization in doing so.

Lacking this influence, the pushing crowd of men concentrated on making their own way displayed in profusion traits distasteful equally to Plato, Cicero, and Thorstein Veblen, not to mention most of the eminent philosophers in between. When some successful members of this horde achieved wealth through speculation in land or in securities or by business enterprise, the difficulty was not so much that they had access to security and leisure, but that they had spent their lives in such a way that they did not know what to do with these advantages. To storm the gates of a social elite turned exclusive because it was already out of tune with a burgeoning democracy perhaps seemed a natural crown for their endeavors, but it could scarcely offer a pleasing spectacle. By the latter years of the nineteenth century the United States had scarcely even the remnants of a landed aristocracy except in the impoverished and defeated South. Business had conquered the nation as business had conquered in Britain, but in this country there were not, as in Britain, surviving symbols and traditions of an aristocratic culture capable of assimilating victorious captains of industry.

America Rejected the Leisure Class

Of course an integral part of the American myth was that the new nation would have nothing to do with a hereditary ruling class or titles of nobility. To most minds, a leisure class of any sort was incompatible with equality and democracy. This resolution had roots in the experience of colonists. For leisure classes are endowed with the power to do great harm as well as good. Being composed of human beings, many of whom are not noble in spirit or intelligent enough to govern others without their consent, they can fall into self-indulgence, corruption, cruelty, or simply unimaginative immobility which resists change whether for better or for worse.

To suggest that a hereditary leisure class is desirable in modern America would be to advocate what the American revolution sought to abolish. A discussion of leisure-class virtue is pertinent only to the question whether it may be possible to nourish in a democratic society the better qualities of the aristocratic tradition—a tradition to which the nation, through its founders and their aspirations, already owes much. They obviously expected, not to plunge a whole population into vulgarity, but to make wisdom and cultivation available to all.

What is gradually occurring, apparently with greater speed as the years pass, is that almost everyone is gaining both in economic security and in leisure. The advantages which in less highly productive civilizations could be enjoyed only by a minority, and by them only so long as they could keep the common herd from meddling with the heritage of the elite, are now being generally shared. For the first time in the history of mankind there is well on the way not a civilization topped by a leisure class, but a civilization characterized by universal leisure. Indeed, there might even be a complete reversal, by which the power would be held by a small minority of hard workers (the scientists, technologists, and professional executives), while the governed majority would have ample time for whatever they wished to do.

The Peril of Democratic Leisure

The unprecedented bestowal of abundant free time coupled with means that in any other age would have been regarded as ample, not on a small class, but on men and women of all ranks and stations, can be a frightening prospect. Power to allot time and energy as one pleases can give scope to creation, but it can also facilitate destruction. Widespread possession of such power represents a challenge not presented to past generations, which had little freedom of choice. The rank and file customarily got the best jobs they could and were anchored to the necessity of working at them. Their lives were disciplined, for the most part, by working routines. Those few exempt from this necessity came under the traditional restraints of their class. If the governing and leisure class went sour—as on occasion it did—it could be thrown out and replaced by another—as on occasion it was. But if a whole people should go sour, who could throw it out, and by whom would it be replaced? It could, indeed, destroy itself, either literally, or by degeneration to something subhuman. The only possibility of salvage in such a case would seem to be some divine operation like the great flood of Biblical legend, in which a worthy Noah had to be found to repopulate the world.

The danger is real, but much of the discussion concerning the threat of leisure is crippled by semantic traps hidden in ambiguities of the past. What is work, and what is leisure? Let us first see if we can put together the common ideas about what these words mean.

Puritan Meanings in Work

Work is commonly used to mean occupation at a job assigned and paid for by an employer. The employer himself may work, but if so his work is what he does to earn money, so that in a sense the customers constitute *his* employer. Individual artisans or professional men or farmers may work without being employed by someone else; but they do so only to earn their livings by selling goods and services to others. Work is therefore a market phenomenon.

Leisure used to mean the time one has apart from work. It may be employed in rest or complete indolence. It may, however, be employed in play. Some forms of play, like tennis or mountain climbing, demand more energy, skill, resolution, and sweat than all but the most arduous of paid jobs. Nevertheless, if nobody pays the player for doing it, it is leisure, not work.

What it all comes down to is that work is felt to be the serious business of life because it is necessary as a means of earning a living. Work is regarded as praiseworthy because it is often not enjoyable, but contributes something others are willing to pay for. Leisure, on the other hand, is occupied with whatever seems most satisfactory to oneself. Customarily it is thought to be in need of justification, and is often excused because it fits one to do better work. Hence the word *recreation*.

Closely associated with this view is the common feeling that if an occupation bores you enough so that you would not do it without being paid for it, it is work; play is anything you enjoy doing enough so that if your needs were otherwise provided for you would do it for nothing.

The traditional economic formulation of this concept is that the worker undergoes the sacrifice inherent in labor in order to enjoy the future satisfaction of consumption, paid for by what he has earned. The employer (or customer) has to recompense the worker by offering him enough wages to induce him to accept the unpleasantness of labor.

Now, this set of assumptions about work and play is heavily colored by the puritanism of the British middle classes, which arose in the seventeenth century and flourished in the eighteenth and nineteenth. The Puritans looked back to the story of the Garden of Eden and found that Adam, because of his sin, had been condemned henceforth to earn his bread by the sweat of his brow. This was a punishment, a divine discipline, which descended to all offspring of Adam and Eve. Furthermore, according to Professor R. H. Tawney and other scholars, John Calvin's doctrine of predestination confirmed the Puritans in their belief that successful businessmen were instruments of the divine will in enforcing labor upon reluctant workers, and indeed in administering the whole money-making and goods-making activity of Western man under capitalistic enterprise.

Puritanism, wrote Tawney, in his *Religion and the Rise of Capitalism,* "was the schoolmaster of the English middle classes. It heightened their virtues, sanctified, without eradicating, their convenient vices, and gave them an inexpugnable assurance that, behind virtues and vices alike, stood the majestic and inexorable laws of an omnipotent Providence, without whose foreknowledge not a hammer could beat upon the forge, not a figure could be added to the ledger."

Lewis and Angus Maude, in their study of *The English Middle Classes,* asserted that "the Puritans made life in many ways a good deal less pleasant for the poor by interfering with their leisure; official displeasure ended many, though not all, of the traditional sports, festivals, and pastimes which had lightened labor and given dignity and meaning to life. . . . They imparted to the English mentality a strain of gloom, a sense of guilt, and struck an almost fatal blow at the nation's artistic powers. . . . The Puritans set in motion psychic forces which were to usher in the middle-class age of ugliness, desecration, and aesthetic insensibility in years to come. Determined to live frugally themselves, and to keep sin at bay by ceaseless business, they sought to refuse pleasure to everyone else. Their monument, their sacred legacy to posterity, was the English Sunday."

Undoubtedly men will not willingly submit to the industrial discipline of wage labor without a stronger compulsion than mere financial incentive. American businessmen operating in more primitive societies have often observed that the people of non-commercial cultures cannot be induced to produce more by higher wages; they may accept more by the piece, the hour, or the day, but in consequence take more hours or days off. A moral compulsion to work and to get ahead appears to be necessary in the mythos of a society if it is to operate

an industrial system with the highest efficiency. The Puritans
supplied this in England and a large section of North America.
They exemplified other virtues too, such as a feeling for justice and the government of law, and personal independence as
against arbitrary power of the state. Yet the bitter essence of
their conception of work lingers in our ethics—it is a duty,
like most duties, unpleasant; and just because it is unpleasant
it disciplines the soul. Any pleasurable pursuit they regarded
for that very reason as vain or even wicked. We have softened
the doctrine just enough to think pleasure, though it may be
permissible or even necessary, ethically inferior to, and incapable of being fused with, serious endeavor.

New Meanings Needed

But do these associations with the words *work* and *leisure*
fit the realities? Many a first-rate mind has worked, presumably with pleasure, and certainly without pay, at creative activities of incalculable benefit to society. Neither Sir Isaac
Newton nor Sir Francis Bacon was hired to do his job; no
immediate commercial demand existed for their labor, because few others knew enough about what concerned them
to demand it. Did Albert Einstein, who apparently enjoyed
his work—though he did receive a moderate stipend—benefit less from it than a laborer who wears his life out early at
digging ditches?

What essentially distinguishes work from whatever its opposite may be is neither that the worker is paid for it nor that
he finds it unpleasant. Even pleasurable work may have its
periods of monotony or routine; frequently it is extremely
arduous and tiring. If a man engages in it without the spur of
necessity, the reason is certainly not that he is indolent and
likes to take his ease. The pleasure to be obtained from it
is the expression of vigor, of purposeful, coordinated endeavor.

To work well a man must first have in mind a goal—the

achievement of a result which seems to him intrinsically satisfying. Nobody works at highest capacity to gain an end chosen for him by someone else. To be sure, the needs of society may and usually do condition the choice of even the most independent worker. The bare need for food, clothing, and shelter may make it necessary to choose to work, but the weakest of motives to work well is that of the person who thinks of his job merely as doing what is required by an employer, or a customer, in order that he may receive a living in exchange. And unfortunately in our civilization many have been able to think of their work in no other way.

Sigmund Freud, in *Civilization and Its Discontents*, wrote: "Laying stress upon the importance of work has a greater effect than any other technique of living in the direction of binding the individual more closely to reality." But Freud continued, "the daily work of earning a livelihood affords peculiar satisfaction when it has been selected by free choice, i.e., when through sublimations it enables use to be made of existing inclinations or instinctual impulses that have retained their strength or are more intense than usual for constitutional reasons."

Dr. Geraldine Pederson-Krag, who has inquired into the circumstances of work under mechanized mass production, does not find in it the virtues pointed out by Freud. It does not bind the worker to reality, she reports—that is, afford him a means of growing up—but instead imposes on him, "first, a return to infantile living conditions, including the realization of infantile fantasies; second, excessive demands for libidinal output; third, a return to childhood emotional relationships." [1] Dr. Pederson-Krag does not disagree with Freud about the salutary effects of work; what she is saying, in effect, is that the mass-production operative is not engaged in work of the sort Freud had in mind. And, though she does not point this

[1] Geraldine Pederson-Krag, M.D., "A Psychoanalytic Approach to Mass Production," *The Psychoanalytic Quarterly*, Vol. XX (1951), pp. 434–51.

out, free choice among numerous occupations probably had little to do with the production worker being in the factory.

"The size and complexity of machines in heavy industry tend to produce in us by comparison a sense of personal inadequacy and of surrounding threat. . . . Though the worker's strength is fantastically increased by machinery, the result of his efforts seems to him nil. However strenuous his work, it does not appear to affect his environment in any way. Mass production demands that the same process be endlessly repeated and each object on which the process is performed moves on to the man responsible for the next operation. The worker sees the unchanged raw material or partially finished products rolling evermore toward him. How different is the work of the handicraftsman, planned and executed in a definite time to accomplish a tangible result.

"Often the sense of unreality which these conditions engender is not dispelled by human companionship. The noise in many factories makes conversation difficult or even impossible; moreover, if the worker is paid on a piecework basis, he must concentrate all his attention on the job to earn a satisfactory wage." Similar divorce from reality, the author points out, exists in many clerical occupations, which become "the performance of meaningless rituals."

Two kinds of reaction are possible. "One type of worker becomes bored with work which has no beginning or end, no reward other than the weekly pay check. He becomes absentminded, prone to accidents or unnecessary absences, and develops hostility to authorities who have condemned him to such tedium. . . . The second type retreats from reality. Daydreaming is to him more congenial than accomplishment, and he finds a haven in the noisy isolation of the factory." He is not unhappy; far from it. But for the moment at least he is passive and finds his escape in retrogression and isolation.

Surely "work" and "leisure," with all the associations clinging to them, are inappropriate terms by means of which to understand the changes taking place in our own civilization. Ruling classes in the past have sought to escape stultifying and meaningless work by imposing it upon slaves and captives. Sometimes they have done so because they loved indolence, luxury, or power, but often because they believed they needed their time for more important or creative pursuits. Even when a wage system supplemented or supplanted slavery the rulers usually regarded the workers as an inferior class unfit for full citizenship. Later, men holding egalitarian sentiments, bulwarked by the Christian faith that all men are brothers, sought to dignify work and the laborer, but not to the extent of granting him social equality. Men may be benefited by the work they do, but seldom by work imposed by others rather than freely chosen, work in which the doer can see no tangible benefit.

Democracy and technology in combination have, almost intuitively and without ever precisely seeing the problem, edged toward a new solution. They have gone a long way, both toward removing the stultifying type of work from the paid worker, and at the same time gradually absorbing him into a universal leisure class by making it possible for him to be free from the job for longer and longer periods. The process will be completed when automatic devices take the place of operators of repetitive machines, clerical drudges, and workers on assembly lines.

Paradoxically, our civilization is clearing the way for meaningful and voluntary work by maximizing leisure. As it does so, we shall either have to abandon the old associations of both words, or have to invent new terms for what we mean. A transvaluation of both is upon us. Perhaps, as a start, we might get rid of the deceptive value judgments by using such simple descriptive words as "paid time" for occupation on remunerative jobs and "unpaid time" for the rest.

9

USES FOR UNPAID TIME

Unpaid time is, theoretically at least, time which the individual may devote to whatever he pleases. As it increases in proportion to all the time available, the freedom to choose how one shall live is much enhanced. Are human beings as we know them capable of exercising with wisdom so much freedom of choice as the advance of technology seems almost certain to bestow upon them?

If a guess had to be made with no more light than was cast on the subject by the morality of the early industrial revolution, the outlook would be dark indeed. The mass of people were regarded as congenitally stupid and incurably indolent, if not indeed naturally wicked. Without the spur of necessity, they would never mold their characters so as to have a chance of becoming productive and social human beings. When family farms or cottage industry were the chief means of subsistence, the authority of the head of the family kept them in line and instilled sober habits. With the advent of the factory system, the discipline of the workshop under an employer, who might arbitrarily deprive any slack or incompetent worker of a livelihood, was substituted for that of the family unit and the patriarch.

Unemployment was regarded as sinful, and the unemployed were thought to be—as indeed many of them through necessity became—vagabonds, roisterers, or criminals, to be shipped willy-nilly from their native lands to new countries where the demand for labor might redeem them. When wage-earners began to ask relief from overlong working hours, a common objection was that, with more leisure, they would turn to bad habits.

During the steel strike of 1919 I heard an old and skilled steel worker testify before an investigating committee that he favored the existing twelve-hour day and seven-day week because it "kept the men out of mischief." Now, after steel workers have achieved a forty-hour week, it would be difficult to prove that drunkenness and debauchery are any more prevalent than thirty-five years ago, or that more subtle changes for the worse have corrupted character. On the contrary, any careful observer in the region could detect what would seem, on any common-sense basis, enormous improvement. Far higher literacy, better housing and sanitation, less corrupt politics, a marked improvement in civil liberties and in citizenship, both political and industrial, are evident. This is not merely because steel workers now have the time, if they wish, to attend church on Sunday. Either they have carried over from the industrial discipline something which steadies them in their other occupations, or American society has begun to prove itself capable of providing a cultural environment in which man need not lose his dignity and significance just because he is no longer compelled to spend all his waking hours in the mills.

That rhymed nineteenth-century maxim for the young—

The Devil will
Find mischief still
For idle hands to do—

seldom provokes in the mid-twentieth century more than a
smile at its quaint odor of antiquity. Most people, whatever
the triviality of their off-job occupations, seem to find enough
to do so that hands are seldom idle. No census has ever classified how the population of the United States occupies its unpaid time, yet a long list of pursuits would certainly be
prominent in any such tabulation. Without questioning at
this point the desirability of these pursuits according to any
criterion except the obvious fact that many choose them, let
us review some of them briefly.

Child Care and Family Leisure

In spite of a long-term falling trend in the birth rate, young
women have recently been marrying early and are having
more children per family than women in the previous generation. Procreation and child care do not fit either of the mutu-
ally exclusive categories of "work" or "leisure." Certainly they
constitute both a productive and a taxing occupation, and
certainly this occupation is not paid for by an employer; no
woman would occupy herself with it for wages. In the later
nineteenth century it could be alleged that most women had
to marry for support even if, left free to choose, they would
not have done so, and that having children was an almost
inevitable consequence of their marriage role. Today neither
of these necessities exists. Young women who marry freely
choose support by a husband in preference to earning their
own way. This is true especially in the upper middle classes.
And women who, being married, have children almost invariably do so by choice.

There are plenty of women who must combine remunerative work with child-bearing and child care, and some who deliberately choose that combination. In these cases the time devoted to the family might be called "leisure," since it is not paid for, yet hardly by any stretch of the imagination can it be less than a major responsibility and an exacting—however satisfying—round of duties. Nursery schools, baby-sitters, mechanized homes, precooked and frozen foods, and shorter working hours have made it easier for the active mother to hold a job without incurring or deserving a charge of neglect. As for the non-working mother, she may manage to acquire a good deal of leisure from her non-paid job by virtue of these modern aids, especially if the family is small and the youngest is in secondary school or beyond. Yet being a housewife remains an important occupation outside the commercial market, which engages the attention of a larger share of the population than is employed in any of the income-earning pursuits.

Husbands, like other members of the household in our modern servantless culture, often participate both in child care and in housekeeping. Many of them have taken up cooking as a craft, at least with special dishes and for parties. Cooking now tends to become, more than in the past, not just a means of providing nutritious food, but an art to please the palate, often with exotic dishes borrowed from extra-regional or foreign cultures. Men, women, and their children of course do much else in and about the home which is productive or even aesthetically creative, but for the moment let us pause to take account of the more passive pursuits.

Passive Entertainment

Aside from the housewives who listen during the middle hours of the day to the dreary and never-ending serial soap operas while their hands are engaged in housework, radio listening appears to be reserved more and more for special broadcasts such as weather reports, favored news commentators, ball games, horse races, public events, or concerts. Children, especially adolescents, may listen to Westerns or mysteries, and at least as often to the latest popular music, approving or disapproving the current top ten or twenty songs, or exercising their critical judgment on jazz, bebop, or the latest incarnation of Dixieland.

The radio has given place in many a living room to the television set, but even this has lost its novelty and no longer commands the rapt attention of so many families for hours on end. Amusement must be high-powered indeed to attract the same audience by use of the same talent day after day indefinitely. There comes a point of diminishing return. Since only rarely do all members of the family like the same program, some are likely to retire to read by themselves. Experts in consumer habits believe that television, instead of inhibiting reading, has increased it, since it keeps the whole family at home, and it bores some of them at least some of the time.

Whatever may be the quality of the matter read, or the ability of the reader to read, there is no question that the gross amount printed and sold is greater than ever. Newspapers, periodicals, comic books, books in covers hard and soft—all are sold in large quantities. Public libraries are crowded. In 1950 more dollars, even after correcting for the rise of the price level, were spent for books than in 1940.

If the figures were available, it might be discovered that many more hours have recently been spent listening to records, including good music, than to TV entertainment. Forty per cent of all records sold in 1951–52—and an enormous number were sold—were of classical music, as compared with 30 per cent before World War II.

This apparently has stimulated the demand for live music. Baseball parks have a more justified complaint of loss of audiences to television than have symphony orchestras; Americans pay more in a year for admissions to symphony concerts than for admissions to ball games. Attendance at serious concerts increased 60 per cent between 1941 and 1951. The number of cities providing regular classical concerts increased from 1000 to 2100 between 1940 and 1951, while in the same period the number of symphony orchestras in the United States grew from 111 to 200.

Motion-picture theaters have, however, suffered. They attribute their slump more to the introduction of television than to anything else, though they obviously have to contend also with parking and transit difficulties, as well as with the competition of all other ways of spending time. The big producers have reacted with gaudier, noisier, and more spectacular productions, presented with new techniques, some of which add perspective. No age and generation has been without its popular devotion to spectacles, absorbed with imaginative participation but without great effort. There is nothing wrong in this, even though one may hope that the spectacle may leave something behind it better than a foul taste.

The legitimate theater, which long ago began to suffer from movie competition and other economic ills, is regarded as being in a sad state. Most cities rarely have an opportunity to see a play with live, professional actors. But at any rate 85 per cent more was spent on commercial types of theater, opera, and dance in 1950 than in 1940. Meanwhile experimental "off-Broadway" performances and summer repertory companies keep the interest in theater alive. The amateurs have their role in this form of entertainment also; something over two thousand community theaters are said to be in operation in the United States.

Active Home Pursuits

As metropolitan regions have grown in size and population, so have suburbs and country living outside suburban areas proper. Much of the time men have gained from hours on the job they now must use in getting to and from the job—on weekdays. But work, even in some large office and manufacturing establishments, is beginning to move away from city frustrations and high rents to the suburban regions themselves. And long weekends have become customary for all. Landed proprietors constituted the aristocracies of the older civilizations; the multitude of dwellers in suburban and country homes are busily engaged in many of the same pursuits praised from time immemorial by the aristocratic philosophers.

Gardening, landscaping, and the like, approved by the classical writers, combine contact with nature, a healthful occupation, a chance to exercise creativeness in love of beauty, and a supply of health-giving contributions to the diet. They are by no means new pursuits for Americans of all classes, but both the proportion of the population which follows them and the time available for the average gardener have increased markedly in recent years. Immense resources of agricultural technology have been released for the use of the amateur grower. Fertilizers, insecticides, tools of modern design, better seeds and plants, and instructional reading matter are all available in large variety. As hired labor has become scarcer the great estate has declined, but simultaneously the small one, on which the householder does all the work, has flourished. Even in the kitchen the deep-freeze and other appliances have simplified the preparation and preservation of fruits and vegetables.

Not only in gardening, but in other pursuits related to the home, people have taken to domestic chores and handicrafts in such numbers, especially since World War II, that the phenomenon has attracted wide attention and a name—the "Do-It-Yourself" movement. One way of illustrating its economic importance, though not its full significance, is to quote the statement in *Time* of August 2, 1954, that the purchase of materials, tools, equipment, reading matter, and the like by amateurs engaged in producing for themselves things that otherwise they either would not have had at all or would have paid for in finished form has given rise to a business of $6 billion a year.

Among other items of information cited by this article (figures which, though they may be guesses, were hardly manufactured out of thin air) were the following:

> In Los Angeles 500,000 persons visited a commercial show catering to "do-it-yourself," and bought, in five days, $1 million worth of equipment and materials from 300 exhibitors.
>
> In 1953 there were 11 million amateur carpenters.
>
> They used 500 million square feet of plywood.
>
> They possessed 25 million power tools.
>
> They consumed in their work enough electricity to light Jacksonville, Florida, for a year.
>
> Amateur painters put on 75 per cent of all the paint used in the United States, and amateur paper-hangers put up 60 per cent of all the wallpaper.
>
> Amateurs laid enough asphalt tile to cover the whole state of Oregon—half of all that was produced in the United States.

These figures illustrate the less ambitious and perhaps the more practical pursuits of those who in their unpaid time have taken to working for themselves. The variety of the things done, however, is by no means limited to repairing, adding to, and furbishing the house. Some amateurs actually build houses, garages, or cabins, with a good deal of help from plans and materials furnished by the businessmen who have found it profitable to do so. Tinkerers experiment with the construction or reconstruction of cars, planes, radio, and television sets. Some design and make furniture, while some even attempt that ancient and difficult craft—the building of boats.

From the utilitarian and semi-utilitarian arts the occupations of the non-commercial self-employed range into more purely aesthetic expression. Amateur or semi-professional

musicians are plentiful. In the early days of the phonograph
and later the radio, the piano manufacturers suffered heavily;
it was thought for a while that pianos might join draft horses
as victims of technology. But pianos and many other instruments have come back. The musicians are matched by those
who work at drawing, painting, the graphic arts, wood-carv-
ing, and even sculpture, often of the mobile or other modern
variety. Perhaps somewhere in the outer reaches of the fine
arts lies amateur photography, the immense and still growing
popularity of which is obvious without any statistical support.

Reasons for Doing It Yourself

Anyone is at liberty to speculate about the causes of these
immensely various preoccupations of a large proportion of
the population. There are some, however, that can scarcely
be questioned.

As technical progress has raised wages in the more highly
mechanized industries, and the wide extension of purchasing
power has kept employment high, wages have risen also in
home building and maintenance, domestic labor and other
largely handicraft occupations, without the corresponding reduction of labor cost per unit which advancing efficiency
brings to industrial establishments. Casual labor available for
individual hire, aside from being high-priced, frequently cannot be obtained at all. This situation supplies a strong economic motive for the individual to do as much of his own work
as possible, and to make things he cannot afford to buy.
There seems little probability that the trend will be reversed.
The American, and particularly that kind of American called
Yankee, has always been known as an inventor, a putterer, a
Jack-of-all-trades. In the United States there has been little
social inhibition to prevent anyone from doing any kind of
chore he pleases. Craft demarcations have never been tightly
frozen into castes or social classes. Nothing could be more

traditional, when occasion arises or strong motive exists, than for an American to try something he has never been trained professionally to do.

A high degree of emotional satisfaction can be obtained from working at, and finishing, an object which not only has utility and can give pleasure to the owner but represents to him a coordinated physical and mental effort which results in visible achievement. This type of satisfaction is denied to millions in the work for which they receive pay from employers or customers. Probably many do things for themselves from motives which they regard at the beginning as purely utilitarian, but continue because they find it as good fun as anything they have ever done, and moreover a welcome release from the tension and routine of working for a boss.

Whatever the springs of human energy tapped by this remarkable new development, it is surely as spontaneous as any form of behavior can be in modern civilization. No pressure of dire physical necessity or parental or family training, of social compulsion or of political regulation, has led anyone to indulge in it. It was not decreed by the ethics of any religion or quasi-religion. For the most part it is not even a self-conscious search for culture or even health, though it may have far-reaching cultural and hygienic results. It is hardly a cult, or a disciplined movement for the betterment of the world. Each participant has freely chosen to do something, and he has chosen from a wide array of possibilities what he wanted to do.

The opportunity to choose, it is equally certain, has arisen from the development of a technological society, which has supplied at least a minimum of physical necessities, while it has offered the opportunity to use large and increasing amounts of unpaid time in pursuits other than "working for a living." Without knowing what they were doing, or at least without giving it so ambitious a name, the participants have begun to cultivate, outside the world of getting on, what John

Stuart Mill called the arts of living. Each in his own private
way has been enjoying Thomas Jefferson's third great right,
the right to "the pursuit of happiness." And they appear to
have made tolerably good use of that right.

Participating Sports

Probably no people in the world spends more time in active
sports than the American. Some sports are competitive, some
are not, but most involve skill, planning, training, and the use
of the body along with the mind. Generations ago such sports
used to be confined mainly to the young; now they involve
almost all ages and almost all income levels.

So all but universal are fishing and hunting, especially
among men, that those who have in charge the public relations of Presidents of the United States usually advise them
that they ought to engage in these pursuits (and make sure
that their exploits are reported) merely to keep in the public
eye and to show the common touch.

Golf clubs and country clubs, which began to appeal to the
upper income classes in the early years of the century, have
proliferated in suburban regions and are common in public
parks as well as in exclusive neighborhoods. So are swimming
pools and small boat harbors. Sailing is no longer the exclusive
sport of those who can own large yachts with hired captains
and crews but is possible to almost anyone who can afford
an automobile, provided he has the time to care for a small
craft. Motorboats, too, may be had at much more modest cost
than formerly. Winter sports have expanded with equal
rapidity.

Among the most rapidly growing and profitable industries
are those which supply equipment to the very large segment
of the population which actively follows outdoor sports. No
admirer of the ancient Greek valuation of athletic games can

decry the cultivation of the body which is now more wide-spread and better publicized than in any previous age of history.

Seeing the World

Travel has for centuries been recognized as a way to stretch the mind and broaden understanding of unfamiliar phenomena, both human and non-human. Americans have long been more highly mobile within their own country than most peoples, and the omnipresent automobile and motor highway, coupled with time to use them, have multiplied mobility many fold. Testimony to this occupation is supplied by the rash of motor courts recently constructed on all main highways. Automobile tourist traffic has long since penetrated in vast numbers one neighboring foreign nation, Canada, and has begun to reach southward into Latin America.

As for overseas travel, it boomed in the 1920s and suffered a heavy relapse in the subsequent years of depression and war. Since then, however, it has grown as rapidly as the accommodations of steamships and planes have permitted. Moreover its character is changing. Europeans who catered to American tourists before the depression used to concentrate their efforts on de luxe hotels, expensive restaurants, and first-class trains. Now they are discovering that a horde of students and others with restricted budgets are taxing the facilities available to a modest income. Conducted tours are now supplemented by small, self-managed groups of young bicyclists and those seeking temporary residence with European families.

Europeans are beginning to know Americans not chiefly as vulgar and boastful tourists desired only for the money that may be attracted from their pocketbooks but as people. Leisure and means to travel abroad have spread rapidly downward from the type of leisure class that Thorstein Veblen dis-

liked as much as any foreigner. What is more important for
the fruitful use of time is that many of the tourists themselves
are learning to know the people they visit rather than simply
collecting the tiresome impressions of hectic sightseeing.

The motorcar itself, aside from being a mere means of transportation or slick expression of social status, continually
harassed by traffic jams and employed with imminent danger
to life and limb, has recently become to an increasing number an expression of craftsmanship in construction or of joy
in use. The "hot-rodders" began it with their efforts to put
together stripped-down imitations of racing cars; postwar
importations of sport models have revived the earlier interest
in motoring as an exercise of skill. An anonymous advertising
writer, in order to push the product of his industrial client,
strives to exploit this mood. He writes: "The good driver . . .
doesn't ride in this machine . . . he becomes a part of it. It
is a direct, vivid extension of his will, an almost-living thing
that answers a nudge of the toe, a feather-light pressure on
the wheel, with eager precision. The bucket seat molds itself
to his back and through it he 'reads' the road . . . ; he knows
exactly the position of his car, its balance, the grip on the
pavement. No matter how lightning-fast the movement of
hand or foot, the Corvette responds . . . right NOW . . .
and with hairline accuracy. And when he punches those big
brakes it STOPS, in one solid chunk."

Social Production

Utopians always favored the association of workers co-
operatively to produce the world's necessities as a desirable
substitute for capitalist employment. Though there have been
some successful attempts of the kind, as a rule cooperative
producers' associations have not fared well in the world of
business. Meanwhile, almost unnoticed as an economic phenomenon, voluntary associations of people to engage in activ-

ities or to perform services that business will not or cannot do
have proliferated, particularly in the United States. There is
no need to enumerate the enormous variety of such organizations in the work of which persons with well-developed social
talents spend much of their time. Boards of hospitals and other
philanthropies, unions, parent-teacher associations, political
organizations—anyone could extend the list indefinitely for
himself.

Such groups are sometimes futile and some are even meddling busybodies, but without the great majority of them
American life as we know it could scarcely go on. No such phenomenon would be possible in a nation in which there were
not many citizens with time and means to devote to voluntary
activities. It does not exist to anything like the same extent
anywhere else.

Among these groups are many who enrich—or at least strive
to enrich—the aesthetic life not only of themselves but of
their communities. All but the most celebrated and central of
the symphony orchestras contain amateurs who make their
livings at something else but meet regularly to rehearse and
give performances. In some cases these participants have been
or would have been full-time professionals if there had been
a steady enough demand for their services. But many conceive
of their music as an avocation, though it may absorb a major
share of their talents and interest. The attraction of musical
participation sometimes, as in the case of the Vermont Symphony Orchestra, leads the members to make weekend jour-
neys all over the state in order to prepare and produce their
programs. Volunteer choral societies are an old institution, but
recently they have been rapidly growing in number. Chamber-
music groups are a more recent development. The amateurs
devoted to the theater, clustered about community drama
centers, have already been mentioned.

Summer festivals devoted to dance or music may be found
among rural or suburban settings in many parts of the coun-

try. Recently Boston has tried a notable experiment with an annual exposition of all the arts—for professionals and amateurs alike—held in a central location, where any citizen who wished to do so could sample them. The attendance was large and the interest keen.

One must not overlook the organizations devoted either to specific reform programs or to self-education in public problems for the sake of influencing policy. Some are frankly political or even partisan, some are non-partisan although they may engage in lobbying or making specific recommendations. They are concerned with a wide range of social, economic, or political affairs, domestic and foreign. A large percentage of the population, it is true, does not vote, but voluntary efforts to stir an intelligent interest in public affairs wage a never-ending struggle against the apathy of the electorate.

Education Is Booming

The young people of the nation, whether by choice or not, spend much time in school or college which years ago they would have spent on paid jobs. Accounting for both public and private institutions, the Census Bureau estimates that in 1954 there were 1.5 million in kindergarten, 24.4 million in elementary school, 7.7 million in high school, and 2.4 million in college. One-fifth of those who finish high school go on to some form of higher education.

Aside from those in educational institutions at full time, 3 million persons took adult education courses in 6000 public schools throughout the country, and tens of thousands in addition were enrolled in extension or general education courses provided by colleges and universities. According to indications of a sampling study presented to the Adult Education Association in 1954, the most common motive of these adult students was to improve professional skills; the next in importance was cultural advancement. Others wished merely a wider circle of friends or to acquire social graces. The courses given ranged all the way from baby care and jewelry-making to philosophy. The quality of the educational process presumably extended from trivial to the sort of work done by serious students in such an institution as the New School for Social Research in New York. Some adults are so intellectually hungry that they actually matriculate as regular undergraduates in college; doubtless many more would do so if they had the time and means.

Education is not to be assessed by the number of students or the variety of courses. Some of its shortcomings will be suggested on a following page. The relevant fact at this point is that subjection to, or pursuit of, what passes for education is a major unpaid occupation for a great part of the population in the United States. Indeed, the 36 million counted by the Census Bureau constitute a number larger than half the approximately 67 million total labor force—all those engaged in remunerative work, whether as employees, self-employed, or employers. What goes on in educational institutions is even more important, not only to the persons involved but to the whole community, than what goes on in places of employment, since it constitutes the current life of the students and conditions the post-school life of all.

The American population, it would seem, even from a glance at these major categories of occupations off the job, has no difficulty in finding something to do when not in the shop or office, but rather is beset by a host of opportunities, among which the individual may find it hard to choose, or for many of which he cannot find time. And the variety of choices is barely suggested by so short a list. It extends from solitary occupations like bird-watching or other forms of nature study to social pursuits like attending parties, dancing both round and square, taking part in fraternal, professional, or political conventions, going to church or engaging in other religious activities, gambling, playing card games or chess, even (rarely, to be sure) making good conversation. The access of unpaid time has surely had its effect on sex habits, both purposeful and playful, about which not much is publicly or certainly known, even by Kinsey—except for the overt practices of marriage and the family.

What does all this imply for the future of an American civilization in which technology will mature? Not much, except that there are plenty of ways of spending the time unsold to an employer that apparently seem rewarding to those who spend it. There are no ways of delineating that future except by speculation that may be as fanciful as the early navigators' maps of unexplored regions, replete with unknown seas, imagined coastlines, terrifying monsters, and round-cheeked faces puffing the supposedly prevailing winds. There are no ways of assessing the worth of that civilization except by applying to its expected outlines whatever criteria of values the imagining observer happens to hold.

10

THE NEW INSTAR

What kind of civilization lies in the further reaches of the technological revolution as manifested in the United States of America? What is it that Americans are seeking, now perhaps half consciously, in their historic concern with making and consuming more goods in less and less time, and perhaps will seek more deliberately in the future? Will their direction lead to a society that can be ranked with the great ages of the past?

No answer can be more than a series of intimations. Some of the possibilities, however, seem more likely to be realized than others.

The "Static State"

The material basis of the new instar of Western civilization is likely to approximate the goal most fully outlined by John Stuart Mill as "the static state." Mill, like other critics of the

early industrial revolution, hoped that gains of population and
of production would someday cease to be regarded as the
chief end of man. Competitive pushing and shoving in order
to get on by accumulating material wealth, he argued, should
cease to be the means by which the ends of man are achieved.

Population growth in the United States is indeed likely to
diminish, or even to cease, before the land is so filled with
cities, factories, and farms that there is no longer any wild
shrub or plant or any place where a man can be alone. The
production of the material goods that people can eat, wear,
or live in has so much increased, and is likely to make such
further advance, that one want after another will be satisfied;
output of goods will then grow no faster than the population.
Even the quantity of goods used in non-paid time (leisure or
recreation) will impinge on the limitation of time itself. As
material wants approach satiation, the struggle to pile up
material wealth will lose much of its point.

The economists, past or contemporary, who have warned
against the static state have identified it as lack of economic
growth in a populous country which either had not experienced the industrial revolution at all or had faltered during
its course. Adam Smith, in discussing the matter, used as his
horrible examples China, where "progress" had ceased and
consequently average levels of living remained low, and India,
on the down grade in production, where the pressure of population was periodically pushing the country over the brink of
famine. Those prominent American economists who in the
1930s thought the United States, having reached "economic
stagnation" or a "mature economy," was doomed to suffer
continual and growing unemployment unless government intervened to maintain expanding output, were confronting a
society in which at least 10 per cent of the labor force was
unemployed and large sections of the population were "ill
fed, ill clad, ill housed." John Stuart Mill's static state, on the
contrary, would be one in which the industrial revolution had

been pursued far enough so that all could be reasonably assured of what they needed. To achieve this state, even in the United States, will yet require decades of hard work, shrewdly considered public policy, and well-distributed increase of material output.

Mill, of course, used the words "static state" in a strictly limited material sense. He did not expect that man, or his ideas and desires, would become static. Indeed, he intensely desired the opposite. "Mankind," he wrote, was in "a very early stage of development." Technological advance itself would, he expected, continue, but would be devoted to its proper purpose—making work easier. It already has done so. The development of man would be facilitated also, he pointed out, by a marked shortening of working hours. This trend has already become well established and is almost certain to go much further.

Other potential results of technology and engineering, not anticipated by Mill, have already gone far and are likely to be more emphasized as the desirable form of the static state is approached. One is a shift in the kinds of work to be done and hence in the major occupations of the labor force. Backbreaking unskilled labor has not only been made easier; it is gradually disappearing. Monotonous, routine work in factories, farms, offices, and merchandising establishments is now rapidly being taken over by machines. There is, on the other hand, an increasing need for people with training, skills, and ingenuity in devising, building, and adjusting machinery, in the professions, in managerial posts, in dealing with other people. Work on the job, in other words, is being sorted out to impose the more machine-like, deadening tasks on machines, and to leave the more man-like, enlivening tasks to human beings.

Technology is capable of saving not only labor but material resources which are limited in quantity. It can substitute relatively abundant energy from the atom or the sun for exhaustible coal and oil. It can make more efficient the uses of whatever metals or other supplies are needed. It can multiply the output of food per acre. These and like triumphs can stretch the means of subsistence. At the same time science and its applications enable man to limit the growth of population. Limitation of population growth to a pace slower than the increase of the food supply, which looked to Malthus impossible except by heroic restraint, and to Mill desirable though difficult, has become almost an automatic accompaniment of economic growth.

Immense tasks for technology remain, not merely in augmenting production faster than population grows, but in making life as a whole more pleasant and rewarding. None of these tasks is of more moment in the near future than redesigning and rearranging the places where men live. The task has made headway in the individual home at its best; something has been done in the more fortunate suburbs, though here new problems are created almost as rapidly as old ones are solved. In the great metropolitan regions the labor seems like that of Sisyphus. Many of these areas, like New York, are rapidly strangling themselves by multiplying places to sleep and work faster than decent or efficient means of getting to and from them. Of course the problem is not technically insoluble; its solution must await a more widespread will to solve it, less opposition from vested interests, better social and political organization. The technical skill which made the skyscraper is not incapable of designing a setting for a tolerable urban community. In the meantime all those individuals who can do so—and their numbers are increasing daily—are bringing pressure on the overgrown centers to change for the better by the simple expedient of deserting or avoiding them. When great cities, like the economy as a whole, become static in terms of mere magnitude, there will arrive at least the opportunity to improve their quality, and the quality of life within them.

Easier and less work, more economic security, less rivalry
for material success, seemed desirable to Mill not only in
themselves but for a purpose—what he called in one passage
cultivating "the graces of living" and in another learning "the
Art of Life." The conditions which he thought necessary for
pursuit of these ends are indeed being more closely approximated. But is finer quality really being substituted for greater
quantity? Or is the dynamic thrust of a technological civilization merely being transferred from making more things for
more people to doing more things in more unpaid time? Is
there discernible any genuine refinement of values, any more
discriminating choice of ends? Or is there, on the other hand,
a deterioration, as some observers of American society fear?

The Weight of the Average

Classic philosophers believed the laborers and the tradesmen unfit to exercise the duties of citizenship or to pursue
literature, philosophy, and the fine arts. Laborers and tradesmen were in consequence excluded from the governing elite,
or what came to be called the leisure class. The aristocratic
tradition has long since succumbed to democracy: workers
and tradesmen now have political and even social equality.
The modern way turns out to be to diminish the labor rather
than to exclude the laborer, to bestow leisure and education
on all rather than to reserve them for the few.

The classical aristocrat would have expected this turn of
events to debase taste, vulgarize intelligence, and make life
easy for the demagogue, because he thought those engaged in
work and trade were by birth inferior beings, not just ad-
versely affected by their circumstances. Democracy would
dilute the cultural brew to insipidity, perhaps even poison
it. Traces of this attitude are often found in modern critics
of American society, though usually these critics are too well
informed—or too discreet—to put the matter in such crude

terms as supposed lack of blue blood in the multitude. It is
the size of the audience, not its composition, that is blamed
for inferior taste; the generality of the electorate, not its
lack of intelligence, that robs politics of meaning and urgency.

The old suspicion of the tradesman is now transmuted into
attacks on promotional salesmanship of mass-produced articles, of mass-produced entertainment, of political candidates
and parties. To produce cheaply for all it is necessary to em-
ploy expensive means. It is necessary therefore to appeal to as
many as possible in as short a time as possible. The enterprise
will not succeed unless one exploits the impulses that lie
nearest the surface of great majorities. Crude fears, hopes,
desires, excitements that may be shared by almost everyone
must be emphasized, instead of the more carefully reasoned
reflections and the more cultivated tastes that may be peculiar
to the several numerous minorities and even more numerous
individuals of which the great crowd is largely composed. So
the originators, the creators, the dissenters, the leaders with
worth and character, are lost in the average; often they cannot find an audience or a following at all. There is, so it is
often said, in modern culture a social law like Gresham's law
of money—bad currency always tends to drive good currency
out of circulation. Increase of income, security, and leisure on
the part of almost all do not automatically remedy this situation but may even make it worse.

The Case of Books and Reading

In the case of books the situation has been well expressed
by a publisher (The Dryden Press). Gutenberg with his
movable type introduced the written word to the millions, but
the ultimate outcome he scarcely could have conceived. It is
now economically impossible "to publish a book that has great
intrinsic value but that will appeal to a limited audience. . . .
The economics of the situation are painfully simple. The

modern book-printing press operates at a speed of about 3000
impressions per hour and prints 32 or 64 pages per impression.
But each 'form' of 32 or 64 pages must be carefully 'made
ready' before the press starts running, and this makeready
may take from four to twelve hours per form, depending upon
the complexity of the text. Obviously, devoting several hours
to makeready when the press must run for only 30 minutes is
economic insanity, although the same amount of makeready
time becomes negligible on a printing of 50,000. The same
ratio holds true of the other phases of book manufacture.
Folding, trimming, and case-making machines turn out work
at incredible rates—rates so high as to be impractical for
small editions."

Many publishers, to their credit, do publish books destined
for small circulation, either because they believe that the
authors may come to be profitable investments in the future
or because they like the books well enough to subsidize them
out of their profits. A publishing house, too, may acquire
prestige by including in its list distinguished books which
have small sales. Yet the economics of mass production and
distribution narrowly limit the freedom to indulge in this phil-
anthropy.

The same techniques of mass production that have rendered
small editions unprofitable have also made it possible to sell
enormous quantities of paper-bound books at low prices.
These books range from sex thrillers and crime stories to great
classics and excellent modern fiction and non-fiction. The
great public can choose almost any kind of fare it likes—and
it chooses solid food as well as the non-nutritious or even
poisonous. The complaint is not that the mass of readers do
not have the chance to broaden or cultivate their tastes, but
that the economics of publishing tend to dry up at the source
the new, the unusual, or the meritorious work which for one
reason or another may appeal only to a small public, at least
for a time.

The author of a book which happens to be popular may make money quickly because of a book-club adoption, movie or dramatic rights, and other subsidiary sales. If a paper-back publisher reprints a book the author may receive a substantial sum, though not usually so much as he would have been paid for work of equal difficulty and quality in some other profession. But these are the unusual cases. Meanwhile the competition of cheap reprints may make it even harder than before to sell books in hard covers that do not hit the jackpot. "Most novels," writes Malcolm Cowley in *The Literary Situation* (of the 1950s), "didn't reach a sale of five thousand; they were losing ventures for the publisher and for the author as well. The average income from writing books was below the average income of Southern mill hands, and not much above those of cotton sharecroppers. An author might work a year or more on a book, have it published and favorably reviewed, and still not earn enough royalties to cover the thousand dollars that he might have received as an advance. His next book might take another year and not be published at all." As for the poets, in the United States "only two of them earned a livelihood by writing poetry; one was Robert Frost (who also lectured), and one was Ogden Nash." After writing this Mr. Cowley discovered another one—Oscar Hammerstein, librettist of *Oklahoma!* and *South Pacific.*

The argument certainly is not that every aspiring writer ought to be assured a decent living from his literary work, or that new and good writers do not occasionally make their appearance and find a public. The argument is that mass production and mass reading put such a heavy premium on the recognized and the standardized that there is a subtle but persistent tendency to stifle the biological "sports" in literary creation who, in a simpler society, less heavily weighted in favor of the quickly favored and the popular, might have turned out to be geniuses. If in fact this is happening, we never may have a chance to discover it.

The Case of Music, Drama, and Art

In music, as in reading, there is an enormous and growing audience, and the audience is catholic in its tastes. Democratic appreciation of music shows little sign of ruining the taste of the listeners. Those who begin with a great classic like Beethoven's Fifth go on to compare the rendition of it by various orchestras and conductors, and go on from there to listen to much less familiar works.

Yet never has it been harder for the professional musician to make his living by performing music, never more difficult for a contemporary composer to find a following—or even to get a hearing. While some $200 million worth of records are sold yearly, in 1954 only 74,000 of the 249,000 members of the American Federation of Musicians had full-time work. We need not mourn too much the disappearance of small bands in theaters and movie houses, but the professional symphony orchestras operate at huge deficits; the expansion of symphony concerts is usually at the cost of employing professionals only part time and filling in with amateurs. Some concerts are supported by the AFM Music Performance Fund, derived from a share of the proceeds of record sales.

Rent of halls is expensive—even prohibitive in large cities —except when the concert is subsidized or the seats can be filled at good prices by the attraction of a headliner. Soloists can rarely find bookings except through commercial agencies, which naturally prefer to exploit the big names instead of taking a gamble with new talent. As for the composer, he rarely derives income from either sales of music or royalty from performances unless by some lucky chance he is already well known. He is, economically, even more unfortunate than the literary man.

It is an old story that the commercial theater has suffered from competition with the motion picture. Meanwhile rents and wages of stagehands have continued upward. Only the reckless producer will take the gamble of investing the money necessary to produce a play on Broadway unless he is morally certain of full houses and long runs. And what other cities see is what Broadway has produced. The local theater in the small city—often in the past called the "opera house"—seldom if ever shows a play with live actors, let alone an opera. It has installed a screen and a projector.

As for the movies, they have long engaged in expensive productions that cannot be profitable unless booked widely. We are informed by Arthur Mayer in his "Hollywood Verdict: Gilt but Not Guilty"—a chapter in a recent book, *Is the Common Man Too Common?*—that "the average Hollywood feature film to return its investment must be seen by at least fifteen million people." There are, he writes, less than five hundred theaters that play foreign films or their few American counterparts with reasonable consistency, and they are not widely distributed. Nearly one-fourth of them are in the New York metropolitan area; "they exist in only seventy communities and they represent less than 3 per cent of the total number of theater seats in America." Theaters in small communities, where long runs for any picture are impossible, cannot find enough "art films" or enough customers for them to afford to abandon a strictly commercial policy. There is, it appears, little opportunity for minorities of taste to see the pictures they would most like unless by some leap of nature they become majorities.

How about radio and its offspring, television, which have contributed to this sad state of affairs? We have it on the authority of Gilbert Seldes in the same volume in which Arthur Mayer writes, "that they are for the most part aimed at the same intellectual level and call for the same emotional responses, the level and the responses being relatively low." Mr. Seldes thinks the television broadcasters create the audiences for whatever they choose to present and that, like radio broadcasters in the past, they could find audiences for better things if they wanted to take the risk. But apparently they usually don't. Their costs are too high. "The pure sustaining program of radio, experimental and not intended for sale, has disappeared, and the status of television may now be described as "commercialism mitigated by foundations." Philanthropic experiments *can* get time on the air—if they will pay the bill.

It is almost impossible to reproduce satisfactorily by mass methods paintings and sculpture. The difference between the original and the copy is far greater than the difference between live and "canned" music. Consequently painters and sculptors have not suffered much competition from mechanical duplication. On the other hand they have been unable to draw much income from reproductions, as have successful writers and musicians. A few lucky ones have found patrons, dealers, or museums to buy their work, as in the past. Thousands of spectators crowd the museums and art shows. But it seldom occurs to the individual consumer, even the man of some means, that he might actually *buy* a new picture, even if it is much cheaper than a new car or a mink coat. Without the guidance of advertisement or standardization, he doesn't dare to trust his judgment or indulge his taste. Of course, in the United States he never did. Mass production and mass consumption have not inhibited appreciation of visual art, but perhaps the consumer habits formed by folkways of the mass market place have made it harder for the artist to make a living—as one might expect him to do in a rich and leisured civilization.

The Political Man and Security

Political democracy in the United States has been analyzed many times and in much detail; its faults are as familiar as its virtues. The present generation of critical writers has much

to say about at least two democratic dangers that are new, or
at least newly prominent. Both are closely germane to the
subject of this book, since both stem in part from the advance
of science and technology. One is the possibility that political
opinions may be standardized on a low average level, as tastes
may be, by mass communication. The other is that we may
lose both our political competence and our liberties by official
regimentation which uses fear as its whip.

The citizen used to receive his information about public
affairs and his hints as to what to think about them both from
his own experience and from many miscellaneous sources,
varying from locality to locality. He could go to political meetings, take his pick among a number of newspapers represent-
ing a variety of editorial biases. Perhaps, even, he listened to
street-corner orators. Anyone with a cause could start a period-
ical or at least print handbills. Public figures of many sorts,
both local and national, played roles in forming "grass roots"
attitudes—ministers, lawyers, barbers, anyone who could use
a cogent phrase or had a mind of his own.

But expensive mass production is said to have changed all
this. Only the biggest cities have more than one daily newspaper, either morning or evening. The high cost of fast modern
presses, of newsprint paper, of labor, have made all but the
big circulations uneconomical, and, even more serious, un-
attractive to mass advertisers. Whatever news the newspaper
chooses to print, what it headlines on the front page, how it
slants its treatment, determine the kind of news most people
read. Moreover many of these newspapers belong to "chains"
under one or another ownership. Virtually all of them use
syndicated columns or "boilerplate" material. The columnists
do often disagree with one another, but there are relatively
few of them.

The same economics applies to periodicals. The opinions
and interpretations supplied by the mass-circulation media
cover the country; to maintain their popularity they must

appeal to a wide and moderate average. Anyone can lose money rapidly by trying to start a new magazine; his "break-even" point cannot be less than several hundred thousand readers. The small-circulation or variant publications must subsist on subsidies of one kind or another. In seeking to influence public opinion, the publisher can seldom any longer start small and gradually grow big. He must be born a giant, if at all.

Meanwhile the usual voter derives most of his political know-how, not by doing anything—not even attending meetings, conversing, or reading—but by sitting in front of his television screen, seeing and hearing precisely the same things that everybody else sees and hears. No doubt he is better informed than most voters of a generation or two ago. He does see and hear opposing candidates and their spokesmen. But the criteria according to which he makes his decisions, the material for his mental constructs, now come to him ready-made—more than, as formerly, from his direct and individual experience. And when election day arrives he is as likely as not to play golf or go fishing, participating in the contest only to the extent of listening to the returns as if it were merely a political version of the world's series.

The advanced technology of warfare, at first designed to frighten enemies, has now succeeded in frightening everybody. "Security" measures, applied during World War II to prevent other nations from discovering the terrifying secrets at our disposal, did not long prevent that discovery. Spies played a part in the leakage of information, but the scientists inform us that there is no such thing as a scientific secret, or cannot be for long, since the basic knowledge and the arts of discovery are a common human property. It is of course the government's duty to frustrate spies, but we are more likely to hamper our own advance by security measures which interrupt the necessary interchange of scientific and technical information than to prevent the enemy from learning what we

know. Nevertheless, now that atomic weapons are no longer
anybody's secret, "security" continues to be an obsessive concern of government, some politicians, and many citizens.

In the 1920s security meant a bond or a share of stock. In
the 1930s security meant some assurance against the hazards
of unemployment or old age. In the 1950s security primarily
means the effort of the government or even the private employer to fire, or to refrain from hiring, anyone who is suspected of having had the wrong opinions or associates. Security in this sense is supposed to protect the citizen, through
his government, from foreign enemies, but as it often is applied it eviscerates his security as a political man.

So much has been said about this subject that detailed
exposition of the ugly record is scarcely necessary. The relevant point for the present argument is that the resulting in-
timidation may induce prudent people to express no opinions
about public affairs, attend no meetings, belong to no organizations, and avoid knowing anybody who someday possibly
could be suspected of political activity which might fall into
disrepute, lest he be cited in the files of the secret political
police. Nothing could be better calculated to reproduce at
home the regimentation practiced by totalitarian tyrannies,
against whose poisonous influence this enormous apparatus of
"security" was first erected. If that result has not occurred in
the United States—and obviously it has not widely occurred
—the reason is that enough Americans are just not that prudent, and still care enough about political liberty to take risks.
Unfortunately, however, most of the businessmen who spon-
sor radio and television shows, and produce moving pictures
or entertainment of other kinds, are not willing to take this
kind of risk. Personally they may have no objection to em-
ploying persons against whom charges have been leveled
(whether justly or unjustly), but commercially they shrink
from arousing protest from any part of their audiences.

Judge Learned Hand in a recent article referred to "our

constant recourse to the word 'subversive,' as a touchstone of
impermissible deviation from accepted canons. . . . Contrast this protective resentment with the assumption that lies
at the base of our whole system that the best chance for truth
to emerge is a fair field for all ideas. Nothing, I submit, more
completely betrays our latent disloyalty to this premise, to
all that we pretend to believe, than the increasingly common
resort to this and other question-begging words." In another
passage Judge Hand comments that we might be happier
"under the spell of an orthodoxy that was safe against all
heresy." But, he continues, "the best answer to such systems
is not so much in their immoral quality—immoral though they
be—as in the fact that they are inherently unstable, because
they are at war with our only trustworthy way of living in
accord with the facts. For I submit that it is only by trial and
error, by insistent scrutiny and by readiness to re-examine
presently accredited conclusions, that we have risen, so far
in fact as we have risen, from our brutish ancestors, and I
believe that in our loyalty to these habits lies our only chance,
not merely of progress, but even of survival." Many other leading Americans have refreshed our memories about the function of civil liberties, but Judge Hand is singularly worth
quoting because it was his decision from the federal bench
that opened the way to conviction of Communist party
leaders for conspiracy, under the Smith Act. If he believes
that government has the right to thwart Communist conspiracy against liberty, it is not because he would tolerate the
undermining of liberty from any other source or in the service
of any other authoritarian system.

The Case of Education

If tastes for anything but the average and the accepted
are being starved for lack of stimulation, if political life is
being watered down by fear of nonconformity, if courageous

leaders are not being trained, does the hope lie in education—
since the time of Thomas Jefferson conceived as the means of
making possible intelligent citizens and complete men? What
is the condition of education, on which America has so long
staked its democratic future? In spite of the large and increasing numbers in educational institutions—perhaps because of these numbers—the critics make disquieting comments on this sector also.

So small a part of our physical resources has been devoted
to education that the shortage of classrooms is expected to
become 450,000 by 1960. As the great army of children born in
the 1940s has been advancing into the schools, the supply of
teachers has actually been declining. In spite of the shortage,
teachers' salaries are scandalously low. President A. Whitney
Griswold of Yale states that in the fall of 1953 the projected
need for additional properly trained and qualified elemen-
tary-school teachers was 160,000; our colleges in the previous
year produced only 36,000. As the secondary-school enroll-
ment rose (it will soon be doubled) the training of secondary-
school teachers declined steadily in the four years 1950–1953
from 86,000 to 55,000 a year.

Lack of quantity we know how to remedy, and doubtless
will proceed to do so; more serious is what many believe is a
deterioration in quality. Talk with faculty members of any
liberal-arts college—who also are too few in number, without
adequate facilities, and underpaid—and you will be told that
many students are passed on to college without even the
elementary skills supposed to be the basis of education. Some
cannot add, subtract, or cope with the simplest mathematical
reasoning. Some cannot spell or construct a grammatical
English sentence, to say nothing of writing with clarity and
effectiveness. Some are ignorant of the basic traditions of our
culture; they are vague not just about the classics, but even
about American history, to say nothing of European. Some
cannot read well enough to understand or keep up with college

assignments. We have it on the authority of Malcolm Cowley that "an Eastern university that chooses the best from a long list of candidates for admission gave a reading test to its students on two occasions, twenty-five years apart. The test showed that freshmen could read as well in 1925 as seniors in 1950." Lack of ability in mathematics, writing, and even reading may sometimes be patched up in college, but the need to do so is deplorable in view of the well-founded belief that good mathematicians and writers often show their highest competence in the early twenties, if not before.

In addition, many colleges and universities are not performing properly their own educational jobs. In most large institutions classes are enormous, instruction is routinized, without much personal contact between student and teacher. Curricula have run off into fringe subjects, where, under the elective system, students may browse without ever acquiring either the basis or the breadth of a liberal education. Professional schools specialize; they turn out, with graduate degrees, engineers, agronomists, economists, chemists, teachers, or what have you (not enough, to be sure), but many of these are not literate either inside or outside their specialties. One reason college students cannot write is that in their textbooks they encounter so much awkward English and almost incomprehensible jargon, produced by many of the specialists who are supposed to teach them.

Clearly mass production does not work in education. As everywhere else, an effort to strike an average curbs and deprives the exceptional. Many scapegoats have been blamed for the current state of affairs. Guesses include the allegation that children now spend too much time listening and looking instead of reading, that they are led to devote too much effort to learning to "adjust" or pursuing "frills" like social studies and art. Meanwhile defenders of the schools assert, on the basis of tests, that schoolchildren of today are even better in the three R's than those of a generation or two ago. If, they imply, deficiency in these respects appears in college it is only because colleges now admit the culls as well as the carefully selected minority they used to cultivate.

Even the great American philosopher John Dewey and the liberal principles of education derived from his views are attacked by some critics. One gathers that these critics would like to go back to the good old days when children were supposed to learn by fear of punishment, when most of them dropped out of school before or at the eighth grade, and the favored ones who went on were drilled mainly in Greek, Latin, and mathematics. Democracy in education, they seem to be saying, is necessarily a failure and should be abandoned.

More to the point is the comment of President Griswold: "Students who have been hustled through overcrowded and undisciplined classrooms, taught by overworked, underpaid, and improperly qualified teachers, and nurtured on subjects that do not constantly stretch their minds and expand their vision are poor material for college and university." Teaching is an art, to be pursued by those who like it and put into it as much skill and devotion as any fine craftsman. It cannot succeed by assembly-line methods. Education which embodies good teaching is therefore expensive; to offer it to all is doubly or trebly expensive. I speak from experience in saying that education in small classes and with a maximum of two-way communication between teacher and student can be dramatically successful with the average or even the under-average as well as with the brilliant. The United States can have both good and universal education—in time—if the people are willing to pay for it. So far they have not done so, except in unusual instances.

The Background of Conformity

Some sociological writers—in particular David Riesman in *The Lonely Crowd*—argue that conformity or at least acquiescence is favored not just by special circumstances such as those outlined above, but by the broad environmental conditions which American civilization is entering. Riesman's bold thesis is that a civilization which is approaching a static or declining population produces as a typical character what he calls the "outer-directed" man, as opposed to the "inner-directed" man who prevailed in the growing and pioneer America of the past. No brief summary could do justice to his reasoning—which seems to me based on insufficient premises—but the gist of the idea is that now the behavior of the typical American is influenced more by what his associates do than by any inner light derived from tradition and transmitted to him in early youth by the older generation.

An illustration is the new suburban community where the houses, though perhaps different in detail, are based on standardized designs, where most of the inhabitants are within a narrow range of income level and seldom mix with those outside it, where everybody does approximately the same thing at the same time and strives not to be conspicuous by being too different, where both social success and business promotion depend on not attracting much attention except through facility in following well-marked throughways approved by those temporarily exercising prestige. In the 1920s such a community was described by a witty writer as a place "where everybody believes that God is a Republican and works in a bank." Obviously if everybody naturally and voluntarily tries to get along with everybody else by doing exactly what his associates do civilization could stagnate.

Others have remarked what they conceive to be a growing anti-intellectualism. "Eggheads," or, as they formerly were called, "highbrows," have long been subjected to ridicule in our democratic society, but not until recently have they so often been accused of conspiring to subvert hallowed institutions. Aside from the danger that demagogues can play on such hostility for their own purposes, there could arise the

more subtle but perhaps more menacing peril that a population suspicious of ideas and of those who purvey them would
reject the mental food necessary for their further advance, if
not their survival.

Another alarming vista is the thesis that as the technological
complex necessary to sustain the population becomes more
intricate and is carried on by larger units, more controls from
above become necessary. The essential integration will thus
surround the citizen with laws, rules, regulations, and even
control of opinion, so that we may find ourselves in something like Aldous Huxley's *Brave New World* or George Or-
well's terrifying *1984.*

The Meaning of the Dissents

The fact that such dangers to the flowering of democracy
are not mere phantoms of a sleepless night often leads sensitive observers to a quietistic pessimism. No meaningful and
creative period of American history—or any other history—
has been without its shadows and its perils. If no voices arose
to warn against them, to analyze their nature and origins, then
a society might indeed be doomed. Complacency is the all-
embracing danger, just as pride is the first of the seven deadly
sins.

What the protests and the criticisms mean, on a level of
meaning higher than their own content, is that the great debates about aims and policies are being renewed. Not just from
foreign critics, but from Americans themselves, flows in a
rising stream the very type of dissent which has been expressed by thinkers in technological civilization from the
beginning. Questions are raised about the nature of man and
the impact upon him of new institutions and circumstances.
Little by little, issues will be joined, great debates may ensue,
and pregnant decisions may be reached.

A significant shift, too, seems to be occurring in the matters most thought and argued about. The age of the great depression bred a furious concern with the material means of life and their distribution, the organization and aims of economic institutions. Controversy about such matters of course continues and is a necessary accompaniment of successful management of the economy. But it no longer arouses such intensity of feeling or such wide reverberations as in the 1930s. Probably it will not again do so unless the nation is overtaken by another deep economic crisis—an eventuality that most economists regard as unlikely because of the increased knowledge of preventive measures and the apparent will to use them.

What now seems to concern thinkers most is the future of our civilization, the values by which men live, and the cultural development of the individual personality. This is evident enough in the writings of the social critics. And there is ground for believing that it is shared by that large part of the public which reads not purely for entertainment. History, especially philosophy of history which may offer a clue to the future, commands a wide public (e.g., the works of Arnold Toynbee). At present the most popular of the non-fiction books in cheap paper editions are those on philosophy and religion—and not just the religions of the West. At least a million copies of the Koran were recently sold in the United States; there is a burgeoning interest in Buddhism.

It may be argued that all this is merely escapism; people, baffled by the seemingly insoluble problems that surround them, are seeking ways of personal salvation, systems that may provide emotional security and lift the cloud of worry and fear. In many cases this is doubtless true, yet I believe that the prevailing mood is rather like that intended by the death's head, the *memento mori*, at the feast. We live with constant reminders that not only individuals but whole nations may perish in one gargantuan act of violence. Therefore we begin to regard our own lives and the life of our civilization more

seriously. How may meaning and dignity be found while
there is yet time? Can the stamp of eternity somehow be im-
printed on mortality? This is the kind of anxiety, called by
Eric Fromm "existential," which is creative, as opposed to the
neurotic anxiety induced by the ceaseless effort to sell oneself, without perhaps even having a real self at all.

The International Stimulus

If American civilization is to survive long enough so that
the new instar will have begun to take recognizable form,
Americans will have succeeded in living in the same world
with the Soviet regime without incurring a violent catastro-
phe. That awe-inspiring problem is not the subject of this
book. The nature of its solution, however, will condition the
life of the people. It seems likely to be a sort of Missouri Compromise, tacit or explicit, delineating the boundaries between
the two regimes by something corresponding to the Mason-
Dixon Line. Just as the American South was under obligation
not to extend slavery north of the line, while the North re-
frained from abolishing slavery south of it, each of the present
world rivals might gain, at least for a time, reasonable assurance against interference by the other.

In the case of the Missouri Compromise, the unstable factor
consisted of new territories to the West, which, through settlement and development, might become adherents of either
South or North. In the new compromise similar unstable
factors may be found in the "underdeveloped" regions of the
world, in which neither technology nor democracy has made
sufficient progress to relieve hunger, disease, and in some cases
oppression. Thus the American people will be moved to understand these peoples and to strengthen the ties with them, not,
as at present, mainly by military bonds, but increasingly by
economic and cultural means. President Truman's "Point

Four" may, in historical hindsight, appear more important than the North Atlantic Treaty Organization; certainly it could become more broadly creative. And more significant in the long run even than technical assistance or economic aid may be cultural interchange.

It has been suggested that in the next century the concern of the Western world with the continents of Asia and Africa may play a role comparable with the influence on Europe during the sixteenth and seventeenth centuries exercised by the discovery and settlement of America. The influence will of course be of a different kind. The magnetic field in which the attention of citizens of the United States is polarized always included Europe, though the lines of attraction have recently been strengthened by two world wars. Now it has been broadened even further.

The most truly international forces are humanistic leaders, ideas, and aesthetic creations. The gulf between the United States and Russia proves that similar science and technology in themselves, to which both nations are devoted, do not necessarily promote friendship. If in the future the United States produces great men of the democratic and humanistic sort, distinguished literature, music, art, and architecture, and if its political and social institutions evoke trust and admiration, it will do more to justify its civilization in the eyes of the world than any degree of military and economic power, essential though power may be.

Through the texture of daily living, non-prominent individuals may play their part. Even the artistry with which houses and their surrounding gardens are designed can arouse admiration and empathy. For example, the crowds which recently visited the replica of a Japanese house and garden at the Museum of Modern Art in New York went away with a much warmer feeling toward the Japanese than before, in many cases mixed with envy for their taste and skill.

The Avenue of Hope

Is America likely to win world-wide admiration, in view
of the discouraging reports now heard from the critics? What
of the effects of mass production on character, social and
political life, the arts? Does not the necessity of salesmanship
in a commercial order overemphasize a low average and stifle
individuality?

In thinking of such questions one should be careful not to
substitute a cultural or social determinism for the economic
determinism of Marx and his followers, a determinism rejected by the judicious. Environmental conditions in human
affairs are indeed powerful, but not all-powerful. What is
required, if the human spirit is to triumph over almost any
combination of circumstances, is not assurance of success, not
inevitability proceeding from some mysterious force in the
nature of things, but opportunity, however scanty, to mobilize
forces on the side of growth and creation.

Not technology or its fruits limit individual development,
but the way they are used. If purveyors of ideas and entertainment emphasize the average, it is because the market and
salesmanship lead them to do so. The chance to emphasize
the individual and the exceptional, which even now exists
and may become greater in the future, can be strengthened
by the slow decline of dominance by markets and salesmanship. The market culture appears to be self-limited.

As the United States has approached an adequate material
base for a higher stage of civilization, the people, using market mechanisms themselves, and without embracing socialism
or any other named system, have emphasized a growing preference for non-market values. They have done so by un-
willingness to sell all the time at their disposal. Or, to state the
tendency differently, they have increasingly refused to barter
as much of their time as formerly for marketable goods and

services, and have instead retained much extra time for non-commercial pursuits. In this way the relative importance of the market values and of production geared to markets has begun to decline.

It is often said that although the big concerns which dominate American industry no longer compete in the same way as thousands of small producers must compete, they do engage in fierce competition, at least across industrial boundaries, for the consumer's dollar. Actually commercial producers are already competing, and will in the future still more furiously compete, for the consumer's time. After people have a moderate sufficiency of food, clothing, and shelter, their purchases turn more and more to goods or services of which they can make use in their non-paid time. It is in supplying such goods that the most rapidly growing markets now in large part exist. But even here the producers are likely to find that since the time of a given population at best is limited, the limitation of time to use and enjoy goods designed for recreation, "hobbies," and the like will eventually limit their markets. Moreover producers of finished goods are beginning to encounter competition with goods that potential consumers make for themselves, not only because in many cases the maker can in this way acquire something that he could not afford to buy outright, or could not buy at all, but also because he finds so much satisfaction in the process of making it that he prefers to spend his time that way.

Thus the market nexus of the economy, with its values, tends little by little to be de-emphasized by the working-through of the market process itself. This is a gradual and relatively painless type of change. It does not have to be realized by liquidating industrial magnates and shopkeepers and substituting for them employers who themselves are instruments of a dictatorial state, or by establishing state-controlled retail stores where the consumer can scarcely find what he really wants, except possibly at prices that he cannot pay.

In the type of culture characterizing the United States at least, advancing technology progressively allows the individual to exercise more choice as to what extent he wishes to use the market mechanism as a means of satisfying his wants, and to what extent he wishes to satisfy them by direct action of his own. It is not likely, in this culture, that markets and market values will ever disappear in the areas where the citizens show by their patronage that they wish to make use of commercial products. But in areas where commercial products cannot be had so cheaply or are not so good as the things that the consumer can make in his own time, an older type of private enterprise will flourish—the enterprise of the individual working for his own satisfaction. In satisfaction of some wants, products of any sort cannot successfully compete with non-commercial uses of time open to the individual. These include, of course, the practice of the arts, intellectual pursuits, and cooperative or social activities of many kinds.

In the early days of the industrial revolution, competition between the factory-market system and the household system of production rapidly led to the ascendancy of factories and markets because they could make and distribute more articles more cheaply. The commercial order then proceeded to draw many other operations out of the home, like laundry and even the preparation of food. But now the tide seems to be turning. It is not likely to bring back into the household many of the kinds of production that have left it, except in cases where decentralized processing can be cheaper or more satisfactory, as in the case of washing with the aid of machines. But wants that never were adequately met by factory production are finding better expression now that people have more time and means for working with their own hands and brains. This competition with markets by pure but non-commercial private enterprise ought to introduce a more healthy balance into American civilization.

As for the dedicated creators and their access to the public, their feeling of isolation is not new; it certainly preceded the advent of mass production and mass communication. At least since the time of William Morris, many serious writers, painters, musicians, and other practitioners of the arts have felt out of tune with industrial society. While the machine age destroyed the practice and spirit of craftsmanship, factory production corrupted tastes. Producers of the fine arts, and particularly the innovators among them, could only with the greatest difficulty find a market for their wares. If they were without sufficient private means, their sole recourse, aside from abandoning their calling, was to seek patronage, which could be obtained only from the rich and successful or from the state. Some found patrons, but even they were frequently subjected to limiting conditions.

An impression arose that things were better for the creative artist in the Middle Ages or the Renaissance. Then at least the classes and institutions which could offer patronge inherited cultural standards more discriminating than those of most modern businessmen. Likewise popular taste seemed to have been less corrupted by the vulgarities of the market place. This impression may be a sentimental fallacy, but there is no doubt that at least since the Victorian Age the professional practitioners of the arts have as a rule had a tough time, especially in the United States. Something in the civilization seemed to separate the creative spirits from their potential audience; they survived precariously in isolation or in precious cults, while popular taste seemed to pay no attention to them, except perhaps after they were dead and had benefited from generations of publicity spread by the critical mentors of the public.

The ultimate development of technology with its democratic leisure class, however, offers hope that the gulf between the artist and the public may be bridged. In the first place, the creative spirit, as working hours shorten and vacations lengthen, may subsidize himself modestly by occupying paid jobs which still would leave time and energy to do his proper work. In this respect he may be as well off as those in the past who were able to obtain sinecures, like John Stuart Mill as an employee of the British East India Company, or Nathaniel Hawthorne in the United States consular service. A favorite haven of this sort at present is teaching on college and university faculties. This is far from an easy or well-paid profession, but, with its vacations and sabbaticals, at least it does provide opportunities for scholars to pursue their research, writers to write, painters to paint, and thinkers to think. Ingenious and highly motivated workers in the arts have already succeeded in finding varied opportunities of other kinds.

A person who wants more than anything else to write poetry, paint pictures, compose music, dance, or engage in other creative arts therefore is not obliged, and certainly has less need than in the nineteenth century, to make his living by the sale of his product. But what about his audience? Interaction between artist and reader or spectator is an essential part of the creative process. If the book is not published, the picture viewed, the musical composition, drama, or dance performed, it does not come to life. The new society of which signs are beginning to appear bears promise of better publics also. Taste improves and appreciation is sharpened most of all among those who themselves have some experience in creative work. If a large number of people are interested enough in creative arts themselves to produce or perform, the public for the more gifted is almost certain to improve both in quality and in quantity. Eventually this might cumulate in a force that would affect even the great mass-production and commercial avenues of communication.

In the meantime smaller or more local audiences may be found. Technology has even contributed to the mechanics of new printing devices that can produce, not formal books as we know them, but neatly printed and legible copies in small numbers, at negligible costs. There are local and regional art shows, theaters, concerts. Channels are opening between the creative artist and the consumer that are not encumbered by the heavy costs and cumbersome requirements of commercial mass production.

The question remains whether the creators themselves will have profundity, genius, superlative ability. Nothing distinguishes the great professional from the talented amateur more than the extent to which he pours into his work every energy and skill he can muster. The other requirement is of course that he shall have abundant resources within him. To achieve greatness in philosophy, science, art, requires dedication of a high order. What, someone may ask, does this have to do with a nation in which a democratic leisure class has turned to aesthetic or intellectual hobbies? Will not great work and great endeavor be drowned in a flood of mediocrity? Perhaps. But perhaps also average people will more and more come to regard what they can do with their unpaid time not merely as amusement or escape, but also as the serious business of life. That is what they may come to live for. Insofar as they do so, they will have absorbed the mood and the moral standards of the dedicated artist and will be better prepared to perceive and honor his superlative achievements.

As for the danger of regimentation implicit in a high development of industrial technology, we may reflect that as automation proceeds, the regimentation will be of machines and materials more than of men. Those persons who are needed in production of material goods, if they are more regimented than previously (which is doubtful), will presumably have more hours for themselves. The presence of closely packed crowds in cities already necessitates a multitude of rules governing traffic, hygiene, and other forms of behavior, but there is an increasing tendency to escape cities, and technology is making it easier to do so.

Much confusion exists in the old argument concerning cen-

tralization *versus* decentralization. It is customary to assume
that these are exclusive alternatives. But, as the science of
management has discovered, they are, instead, complemen-
tary. By centralizing some functions that can better be performed in that way, more scope is allowed for creative autonomy in other respects. This is the principle already applied
by great industrial concerns like General Motors and Standard
Oil. The householder benefits from this principle also, especially in the country. He may derive his heat and power
from a highly centralized electrical network, or from a gas
line, or from regularly delivered oil. His food and other materials he may buy, if he wishes, at great supermarkets or
shopping centers. His news comes over the air. He can talk
over the telephone. But all this does not necessarily enslave
him; indeed, it may make it possible for him to live in the
country, since he does not have to devote so much time to
the daily necessities of life while he is there. True, he is more
inconvenienced if any one of these centralized services on
which he relies is disconnected or ceases operation. It is more
necessary than before to safeguard continuous operation of
the centralized functions. Like the highly complex human
body, the technically advanced society depends on its nerves
and arteries. One might say that the single-celled amoeba is
more free. But is it free at all, in any human sense?

The Opportunity Is the Goal

Tell almost anyone that there lies in the future a time when
material wants can be reasonably satisfied in a minimum of
time by work that is not unpleasant, that most of life will be
one long vacation in which the individual may do as he
pleases, and he will express uneasiness. A sugar-and-water
utopia with little place for effort and achievement, and little
or no danger, may seem welcome to the tired and harassed,

but after a week or two of it they want, if they are healthy, to
get back into harness. It is therefore reassuring that no future
that can be foreseen is likely to be so placid. The mere fact
that technology may diminish to the vanishing point the need
for engaging in routine drudgery in order to have enough to
eat and to wear does not imply that there will be no other
jobs worth doing, no danger of any kind. On the contrary,
adversity and struggle will always challenge those who wish
to create something unfamiliar or better, whether in physical
terms, in human relations, or in aesthetic creation.

The hardest work of all, many have discovered, is to think.
This is true even in appreciation of what others have thought
and felt. Jacques Barzun, writing in *Harper's Magazine* for
March 1954 on "America's Passion for Culture," declares:
"Whoever says that reading St. Augustine or listening to Beethoven's Opus 95 is the easy, spontaneous way to rest after
a hard day's work at the office is simply lying. Habit makes
artistic attention prompt and pleasurable, but attention takes
mind and physical energy. When I have neither, I read de-
tective stories like my neighbor. So in preaching culture to him
I dare not promise that it will bring the recreation he really
wants; I am asking him instead for more effort, more expense
of every kind, even more worry about the meaning of life."

Some would say that the supreme human achievement lies
in the integration of the unruly self—an integration which,
to be really human, must embrace breadth, depth, variety.
Those who have tried it can testify that this effort is indeed
a struggle of heroic proportions. Others would say that the
chief human objective must be the improvement of the
relationship between the self and other persons, or society
as a whole. The truth, of course, is that both aims are necessary, and that they complement each other. Without the tension between the poles of inner and outer there would never
be either self or society. This magnetic field of force is what

makes it possible to suffuse human life with meaning. Every added degree of freedom for the individual makes the struggle both more difficult and more meaningful.

The challenge in absence of discipline from a boss is to learn to discipline oneself. If work of one kind becomes no longer necessary, the opportunity arises to find work at something better worth doing. Nothing in history would lead to the conclusion that men and women, faced with new dangers, new challenges, new opportunities, must necessarily fail to govern them. The future offers a supreme test to individuals; it offers an unprecedented expansion of freedom, if they will grasp it, to seek the best—as it may seem to them—in their past traditions. By a new renaissance, they may live out these traditions in the new set of circumstances and values. The penalty of failure expressed long ago by Ralph Waldo Emerson in his *Days* must at some time be felt by everyone:

> Daughters of Time, the hypocritic Days,
> Muffled and dumb like barefoot dervishes,
> And marching single in an endless file,
> Bring diadems and faggots in their hands.
> To each they offer gifts after his will,
> Bread, kingdoms, stars, and sky that holds them all.
> I, in my pleached garden, watched the pomp,
> Forgot my morning wishes, hastily
> Took a few herbs and apples, and the Day
> Turned and departed silent. I, too late,
> Under her solemn fillet saw the scorn.

INDEX